The Schoo Member's Guidebook

Every student deserves a high-impact, well-qualified, and governance-driven school board. In this helpful book, best-selling authors Ryan Donlan and Todd Whitaker show you as a school board member how to make smart, worthwhile decisions that will lead to positive change in your district. *The School Board Member's Guidebook* addresses the challenges of making realistic choices that will truly benefit the school and have a lasting impact. Topics include:

♦ How to work and communicate effectively with the superintendent during the year;
♦ How to find common ground with colleagues;
♦ How to represent the interests and needs of the community at large;
♦ How to keep your constituencies focused and informed through strategic planning and structured committee participation;
♦ How to host constructive and cordial school board meetings;
♦ How to capitalize on individual talents and strengths;
♦ And more!

Each chapter offers strategies, tips, and sample scenarios. With these resources and the practical advice throughout the book, you'll be able to make a lasting difference in the lives of every student in your district. You'll be a Difference Maker.

Ryan Donlan is an associate professor of educational leadership at Indiana State University, and specializes in helping schools with leadership and governance. He has authored or coauthored five books, including *Minds Unleashed: How Principals Can Lead the Right-Brained Way*.

Todd Whitaker is a professor of educational leadership at the University of Missouri. He is a leading presenter in the field of education and has written more than 40 books, including the national best seller, *What Great Teachers Do Differently*.

Other Eye on Education
Books Available from Routledge

The School Board Member's Guidebook

Becoming a Difference Maker for Your District

Ryan Donlan and Todd Whitaker

Routledge
Taylor & Francis Group

NEW YORK AND LONDON

First published 2019
by Routledge
711 Third Avenue, New York, NY 10017

and by Routledge
2 Park Square, Milton Park, Abingdon, Oxon, OX14 4RN

Routledge is an imprint of the Taylor & Francis Group, an informa business

Library of Congress Cataloging-in-Publication Data
A catalog record for this book has been requested

ISBN: 978-1-138-31860-1 (hbk)
ISBN: 978-1-138-04943-7 (pbk)
ISBN: 978-1-315-16953-8 (ebk)

Typeset in Palatino
by Apex CoVantage, LLC

Contents

Meet the Authors

Ryan Donlan

Dr. Ryan Donlan helps leaders, teams, and organizations in all sectors move toward personal and professional excellence. Schools and school leaders are his focus. Ryan is an associate professor of educational leadership in the Bayh College of Education at Indiana State University in Terre Haute, Indiana. He leverages leadership capacity in others toward higher performance.

Prior to his university career, Ryan started as a high school teacher and served as an assistant principal, principal, and superintendent over many years in both traditional and nontraditional schools. Leadership development, school reimagination, and organizational wellness are his specialties, as are human behavioral analysis and the study of personality and communication. Ryan is a practitioner's scholar and a scholar's practitioner.

With wide-ranging publications and an expanding readership, Ryan is coauthor of the books *The Hero Maker: How Superintendents Can Get Their School Boards to Do the Right Thing*, *Minds Unleashed: How Principals Can Lead the Right-Brained Way* and *The Secret Solution: How One Principal Discovered the Path to Success* and author of the book *Gamesmanship for Teachers: Uncommon Sense Is Half the Work*.

Ryan is married to Wendy, an early-childhood, infant-and-toddler educator, who is a teacher in the Early Childhood Education Center at Indiana State University. They are the parents of two children, Sean and Katelyn.

Todd Whitaker

Dr. Todd Whitaker has been fortunate to be able to blend his passion with his career. Recognized as a leading presenter in the field of education, his message about the importance of teaching has resonated with hundreds of thousands of educators around the world. Todd is a professor of educational leadership at the University of Missouri in Columbia, Missouri, and professor emeritus at Indiana State University in Terre Haute, Indiana. He has spent his life pursuing his love of education by researching and studying effective teachers and principals.

Prior to moving into higher education, he was a math teacher and basketball coach in Missouri. Todd then served as a principal at the middle school, junior high, and high school levels. He was also a middle school coordinator in charge of staffing, curriculum, and technology for the opening of new middle schools.

One of the nation's leading authorities on staff motivation, teacher leadership, and principal effectiveness, Todd has written over 50 books, including the national best seller, *What Great Teachers Do Differently*. Other titles include *Your First Year*, *Shifting the Monkey*, *Dealing with Difficult Teachers*, *The Ten-Minute Inservice*, *The Ball*, *What Great Principals Do Differently*, *Motivating & Inspiring Teachers*, and *Dealing with Difficult Parents*.

Todd is married to Beth, also a former teacher and principal, who is a faculty member in educational leadership at the University of Missouri and professor emeritus at Indiana State University. They are the parents of three children: Katherine, Madeline, and Harrison.

Acknowledgements

We would like to thank those who have served as "Difference Makers" for us, while we have worked to provide a book relevant to K-12 board members. A special "thanks" to board members Heather Reichenbach from the Warsaw Community Schools and Carol Holzer from the South Ripley Community School Corporation for their prepublication assistance and expertise with our manuscript. Thanks, as well, to the Warsaw Community Schools Board of Education in Indiana for providing feedback on our ideas as we wrote. To our many friends, colleagues, and students at Indiana State University and the University of Missouri, and to our K-12 school partners, we want you to know how much we appreciate your support and encouragement. You keep us relevant. Finally, to our wives, children, and families, we send our gratitude and love for your continual inspiration. We are lucky guys to have you.

1

The Difference Maker

You are a school board member. Whether recently elected or appointed or now enjoying decades of quality service, you have one of the most important professional responsibilities imaginable. Consider the fact that every time you go to the doctor for a checkup, or go to the life insurance agent to purchase a policy that will protect your family, or visit a lawyer to protect your interests in case of accident or injury, or entrust your safety to a police officer or firefighter, you are meeting with someone who had a "difference" made in their lives because of someone like you. Someone on a school board.

Every patriot fighting in our military, every farmer producing food for developing nations, every volunteer helping serve those less fortunate in your community, as well as those investing in the stock market or providing the infrastructure and services to grow our economy, relied upon a quality school experience to get them there.

All who are successful today—or at least most of them—were given the skills to accomplish those feats in school. Folks like yourself were there in governance roles, serving in many instances without the visibility of those in classrooms or leadership capacities, yet in ways that, without your selfless service, quality classrooms and schools would not be possible.

Your governance is crucial. Serving as an effective, proactive, and responsible school board member allows you to make a positive difference in the lives of those who depend upon you: today's children, tomorrow's adults, *and* the adults who are educating children toward a better place in life. And it doesn't end there. The call of board service is in reality a larger investment in one's community. Schools are the second reason—beyond "jobs"—why families relocate to a certain area. Your service on a school board helps answer the question, "What kind of a community are we?" not only within our schools but beyond our school walls as well.

Serving as an effective, proactive, and responsible school board member allows you to make a positive difference in the lives of those who depend upon you.

You are that person who makes a difference.
You are a Difference Maker.
Thank you for that.

Your Role on the Team

Now in order to do just that, you are a critical part of a team that provides the necessary governance and stewardship for a school district to be successful. And your school district may be very small or the size of a city. Either way, the complicated nature of what you are being asked to do and with whom you do it cannot be understated.

Consider the following:

The relationship you have with your superintendent is as complex as it is intriguing. As a group of entrusted community stewards, you hire someone who can be considered a CEO (chief executive officer) of your school district, the lead educator or educational leader. That leader then reports to you because you hold your superintendent accountable for a return on the district's investment. That return is produced in terms of school success and student learning. This seems pretty straightforward.

What is not so straightforward is the fact that, in many cases, you are being asked to govern a school district, and you may or may not have had any formal training to do so. That is precisely the expertise that you depend on in your superintendent for guidance. Other factors in the dynamic here make things even more complicated, such as the fact that, in order to function productively, board members must have productive communication and relationships with one another.

You and your board colleagues may be as small a group as three members or as large as 15 or more. You may have an odd number of members, which may help avoid tie votes, or an even number, which may increase their probability. According to information from the National School Boards Association website (2017), school boards are fairly balanced in gender; roughly three-fourths of them receive no compensation, while others may receive the equivalent of a teacher's pay with benefits. In the United States alone, 14,000 school boards are responsible for *52 million children*. About 95% of the members are elected, with the remaining number appointed. Around three-fourths have at least a bachelor's degree.

Some members work full-time (or more) in other jobs, and board service may be one of their lower priorities, while others may see it as the highlight of their month. And while many board members might have a bachelor's degree or beyond and therefore are likely to be or to have been professionals in their fields, we find at times that, while they have much to offer of their own expertise—helpful to the superintendent and corporation in gaining insight from other professional fields—it can also be humbling for board members to be experts in their own professions, yet not know much about educational issues or school operations. While members might be extraordinarily successful in their own fields, it is hard to be a novice at something, in plain view of all in the public eye. That said, since the year 1647, communities have relied on citizens such as yourself to collectively work to educate their youth (National School Boards Association, 2017).

As a school board member under most state statutes, you do not function as an individual "boss" of anyone, not even your superintendent. The school board as a whole is the unit of authority: a group of people who must function together in a collaborative and healthy fashion in order to make good decisions *as* the boss.

In addition, your group may change every election cycle, bringing new members into the dynamic. The group that you are working with currently may change dramatically within the same calendar year, depending on what happens in any given election or appointment cycle. They may differ dramatically from the previous group, undoing the hard work and direction that had been accomplished.

Some may get along well with others; some may not. Some may bring long-needed expertise with the humble desire to serve. Others may bring strong opinions and visions that differ dramatically from the group you have had in place for some time (despite the hard work you have put in and the direction you have accomplished together).

This can be tough. Or it can be amazing.

Constant change such as this is challenging, for sure. But ironically, it may be the easy part, comparatively.

What can be really difficult is coming to terms as to the best way to balance authority between your board and your school superintendent. It can be a delicate balance, at times, in that in some communities, it is often difficult to discern who is leading whom.

We have heard over the years that schools should avoid having certain persons on their boards of education, purportedly because they can't escape their biases. Examples would be businesspersons with school district connections, spouses of employees, or even parents of current students. We respectfully disagree with this blanket prohibition and believe that these folks can bring great value to board service—that is, *if* (and only *if*) they can see beyond their personal experiences and take measures to avoid conflicts of interest. Their former life experiences may well be valuable, and if considered with the bigger picture, they can help provide the expertise for great governing decisions.

It's all about being able to compartmentalize and have a panoramic view, all at the same time.

Consider the following. We know that if the superintendent is doing too much of the leading, then the board can be deemed a rubber stamp, and nobody wants this. In other cases, if the board is doing too much of the leading, then they are considered micromanaging. This is not good either. Even more worrisome is that in these circumstances, the school board members actually put themselves too close to the decisions that are being made, which can be a negative source of exposure for them that we will discuss later in the book. It can be negative for individual board members, as well as for the integrity of the entire board and, of course, for the superintendent.

In the best possible circumstance, school boards hire trained and educated professionals who can provide guidance and information to a board that functions as a very diverse group of individuals, those who can then see things from a 10,000-foot perspective, a policy-making level, and use their true gifts as "community experts" to make *big* decisions that will have longer-term impact upon the school district.

This is how a school board best exercises its elected or appointed authority and gives the public what it wants: sound stewardship of schools provided for any community, under the law.

What is also difficult nowadays is that it seems a lot of the policy-making has shifted to the state and national levels, stripping the local boards and communities of that power. At times, this can result in boards trying to make a difference with what they have under their control, often focusing on the more minor issues that get in the way of their true governance potential.

To be quite frank, if this is what is happening, the board really needs to ask the superintendent to articulate better the array of important policy-making work the district can still do at the local level in the current environment, given state and national constraints. This may involve a good deal of homework on the part of your CEO, but it is what a superintendent needs to do in order to ferret out the important work that local communities can still get done within the policy-making and budgetary latitude that still exists, even in the most complicated political environments.

This book is designed to assist school boards in best allocating their own talents, governance, and attention, as well as in discerning what they can best expect from their superintendents, so that the optimal working relationship and teaming are possible.

This book is for you—to help you make a difference.

This book is designed to assist school boards in best allocating their own talents, governance, and attention, as well as in discerning what they can best expect from their superintendents, so that the optimal working relationship and teaming are possible.

Understanding Differences on the Board

You'll notice quickly that many of your fellow school board members have varied and diverse backgrounds. They have personal and professional experiences linked with common sense, so they are aware of their strengths and limitations. Others, regretfully, might only have one lens and run the risk of being considered "one trick ponies," who continually have the same limited points of view that affect every decision made.

Some board members have careers in education and may have been teachers, principals, directors, or central office administrators. They may have had long and distinguished careers in education. Nationally, around 17% are former educators (National School Boards Association, 2017). With this former experience, they may be able to lead with dignity and help advance the mission of the district to do what is right by students and staff. Yet please know that there is the possibility that within this group, there may be a renegade or two who didn't have such a positive educational career experience. They may have retired disgruntled or could even have been terminated as employees. They may have an axe to grind and are using the board venue to sink their teeth into something that they perceive needs to be bitten.

Some former educators have a rich experience, which can provide vision and guidance to nonpractitioner board colleagues. With others, their educational backgrounds may be a limitation. They may have had an administrator they did not like, and they see educational leaders through a continual mistrust lens. You don't want to rely too much upon that type of person, which brings up the point that not everyone with K–12 school experience is inherently best positioned to lead a school board in K–12. But you know that.

Other school board members have enjoyed successful careers in businesses in the private or public sector. They bring a delightfully different perspective on how to steward public and private monies and can really diversify the decision-making potential of any group. They may have their own children in the district, or their children may have formerly attended. Some have never had children but really know what kids need and how best to serve them.

No matter the background, let's be honest and say that, at times, we encounter fellow school board members who have difficulty maintaining a district-wide perspective, as they have individual goals that they want to accomplish. These goals may have emotional roots, and we must understand that these persons need to be heard and respected. Some may focus more on sports and wish that we head in a different direction with our coaching staffs; others are more champions of the arts and believe that math and reading now take a disproportional role in a child's elementary school experience. One may feel that we need to put more money into this program or that, yet others may feel that since there's only so much money to go around, giving to some means taking from others.

Seeing the big picture is difficult, for sure, when we bring folks with different personal value systems together and ask that they make decisions as a cohesive unit on behalf of the district as a whole. Yet this is what you, as a board of education member, are being asked to take part in.

Some of you have advanced college degrees; others of you graduated from the school of hard knocks. Yet it's what we can do with this incredible diversity that makes great things possible.

This is where the superintendent comes in.

With no positional power over you as a school board, your school's CEO needs to be counted on to serve as a guide for all of you in order to best represent your constituencies and to make the best possible decisions in terms of the context in which they are being made. Be encouraged to push your superintendent to offer the context your board needs to make good decisions—the "what if?" provider.

We realize that expecting your superintendent to be able to see multiple aspects of every situation is a task that, for the superintendent, might be challenging or overwhelming. But that's what the superintendent is hired to do, and you as a school board should be comfortable in expecting it, so that you can make higher-level and longer-term decisions that will speak well for your district's future.

You may have selected your superintendent after your own election to the board. You may have also inherited him or her from a previous board. Either way, the communication and relationship between the district-level leader and your own school board are critical, as effective governance (the board) must be partnered with leadership and management (the superintendent) to bring about success. Like three legs to a stool (governance, leadership, and management), it is in the board's best interest to remain upright and on solid ground. It's embarrassing for everyone when things topple.

✔ Difference-Making Tips

◆ Difference Makers are honest with themselves and ask continually: "What positive characteristics have brought me where I am today that allow me to make a difference with grace and humility, for those who have entrusted my governance and those who want me to represent them?"

◆ Difference Makers then ask that very same question of someone who will be honest with them in response.

◆ Difference Makers realize that superintendents have the formal training to run a school district operationally and that board members have the community ties that are helpful in allowing a superintendent to develop an understanding of how things work around here.

◆ Difference Makers realize that, beyond community ties, board members have varying life experiences and expertise to balance perspectives and represent diverse viewpoints.

◆ Difference Makers realize that the board *as a whole* has the ability to gauge whether the brand of a superintendent's leadership is a fit for the community and to recognize that it is not really the role of individual board members to make those judgments.

Reference

National School Boards Association (2017). About Us. Retrieved from https://www.nsba.org/about-us/frequently-asked-questions

2

How to Find Common Ground

One board member's thoughts . . .

Whew! A narrow win on election night.

Seems like just yesterday I was encouraged to run for the board.

If I were honest with myself, I'd say that I now feel like the dog that has been chasing the car down the street week after week for a year.

Today, I caught the car.

Now, what the heck do I do with it?!

Note to self: This is beginning to feel a bit more real.

I hope I can make a difference.

When first elected or appointed, you probably were thinking about the challenge of maintaining a common path when your community has such variety of interests and even, at times, demands. We have all had that experience where some of our friends, neighbors, and relatives have wanted us to bring their wish lists to a board meeting, yet when we arrived, we became keenly aware that some of our colleagues were under the same pressure from those very close to them as well, yet with different and opposite viewpoints.

"How are we supposed to navigate that?" you might ask.

Sometimes it seems like an insurmountable task even to encourage folks in any given board meeting audience to "play nice" in public. It is equally if not more difficult to sort through the many voices heard in public testimony, as well as in the community while getting your hair cut, shopping for groceries, or gassing up the car.

We know why there's sometimes a stress-caused tightness in your neck, as people are counting on you to make important decisions that will affect their lives. We bet you have also experienced getting pressure to make a decision that was personally not advantageous for you or your own family and children. There's no easy answer in what to do here, as nobody ever promised you that you were being elected to a position in which there were easy answers and a multiple-choice test key for every "quiz" you felt obligated to take as a public steward.

We can say this, however.

There *is* a general strategy that you can employ to lead amid complexity and to do the right thing more often than not in situations that seem "no-win." The general strategy is to find common ground with others on your team. Find that common thing that you must all do, in terms of advancing the mission of your school district toward the vision of what you can accomplish together, ideally.

And how do board members find common ground? One key is listening to one another, ensuring everyone's perspective is heard. There are likely those in the room who do not have their own emotions tied up in a decision, who are better equipped to study alternative courses of action in a neutral manner. It is important to rely upon one another's wisdom and perspective, and doing so oftentimes results in discussions that are more toned down, with everyone being able to find a common footing.

Though it may seem that such a diverse group as yourselves can vary in thought, opinion, and feeling on what must be done, you are all on the same page on one thing. You desired school board service so that you could make a positive difference in others' lives. This is the blessing of a board with diversity in members and perspectives; diversity makes your board stronger.

You are all Difference Makers.

And your governance role is to help your fellow board members accomplish this *as a unit,* once or more per month, with both positive relations and productivity.

It's not just about what one person can do; it's about what a group of representatives from the community can do to move forward. Power does not come from one individual. If board members present as if it does, the community will come to expect all details to be handled to their specific requests and issues. It becomes a slippery slope when bad precedents are set. It does well to have board leadership remind one another of this.

Working as a unit is key to longevity on a board. If the community senses the board is operating in some kind of Wild West, there is less confidence in the decisions they make, more skepticism in the process, and high anxiety to make sure voices are heard (and often voices that desire to be heard aren't warm and fuzzy, by any means). If people have a sense that the board is even-keeled, data informed, and measured, the board has a much longer rope with which to maneuver through tough situations.

One key to working together well is to understand what each wants individually and affirming these desires.

Please affirm your fellow board members who want to make a difference by cutting taxes. Please affirm your fellow board members who have heartfelt convictions for athletics, the arts, or the sciences. Please affirm those who want to help pass referendums to build new facilities or those who wish that new curricula be piloted. They all have one shared outcome.

They want to make a difference.

Perspectives are critical to understand. Admittedly, you may be thinking that, at times, some of these viewpoints are simply

One key to working together well is to understand what each wants individually and affirming these desires.

unrealistic or ridden with agendas. You may be right. There may be from time to time a left-field perspective or a position statement that anyone with common sense knows would do more harm than good. We understand that. But please keep in mind that board members, especially when in distress, still perceive that they will be making a positive difference if they get their way, even with a blind spot the size of a football field.

One may feel as though she will make a positive difference for her son or even for others if she gets rid of the basketball coach that cut her "little man" from the 6th grade squad. Another may feel he can make an even bigger difference for his community if he gets elected to the school board and then eventually ascends to higher office. Though in some ways their goals may seem illogical, the underlying motive will be such that these persons can make a positive difference in someone's life.

For some with competing agendas, that "someone" might be just a family member. For many, the "someone" might be anyone who benefits from the school board providing a better education for all, which could even have implications for economic development. Please know that the key is to maintain open communication with objectives that are fuzzy, as some "real aims" are obvious, but in other situations, we have difficulty discerning the real purpose in making a difference.

Learning to Make a Difference: Sneak Peek at the Chapters Ahead

A primary purpose of this book is to help you as a school board member understand the importance of using your governance role toward difference making. A second and more exciting objective is to help you develop and embrace the specific skillsets needed to best deploy difference making in the community you love.

To do this in the chapters ahead, we will talk about the constituencies you face and embrace and the challenges that come from mitigating their requests and demands, as well as how you can invest smartly in their passions to get the most return for your efforts. We'll talk about the board of education as a unit and what the focus of our best boards really *is*. We will suggest what you focus your attention on and what you should not in order to get the most efficiency and effectiveness out of your governance team.

We'll also talk about the superintendent as a *shield*, the critical nature of this role, and what you should expect to see as a board unit. This might be one of the most critical things that board members can keep in mind in times when it is tempting to get out in front of the issues that bring about the most passion *and thus the most risks*. Someone needs to have your back, and that someone is, and needs to be, your superintendent.

We'll also talk about the care and feeding of community members. That discussion is worthwhile because, as we all know, when people's basic needs are met, they are typically more able to interact with others. Wouldn't it be nice if all of the folks who approach you as you do your lawn work, while shopping on weekends, or at the local sporting event felt cared for and energized as they relayed their concerns to you and as you responded to what was being done about them?

Sure, it would, and we'll give you some tools for these conversations.

We hope as well that you find our ideas on running board meetings helpful and possibly of help to your board president and superintendent. You are very, very busy, and when you go to meetings, while we believe that the board meeting's focus should be on the business of the school district, we believe that those preparing for board meetings should have that focus. This will position you better to conduct the business that needs to be done. We'll share how all this happens, at least in our minds and experience, ideally.

We understand that board meetings happen only once or twice per month (hopefully), and there are often around 28 or so other days, where you are being asked to do something in your role as a board member. So we have provided a chapter, "Between Board Meetings," with a few ideas on how your life and stewardship can come together in a way that works for you and works to make a difference. It is at these times that you will be in continual contact with your community constituents, so we even provide you a chapter on "Community Caricatures," the typical folks who will bend your ear and ask you to do their bidding—some well-intentioned and others possibly not.

Finally, we talk a bit about "Advancing by Retreating" and "Starting Undefeated," a way to reenergize each year. You may find that your board service and difference making last for many years; conversely, you might find that other challenges call your name and that you need a way to gauge when you could make that transition while "at the top of your game," as they say.

Now that you are a school board member, you are undoubtedly aware of the vast responsibility you have. Each day, your governing decisions influence countless children and adults in our schools. You knew this clearly when you registered interest in service of this magnitude. Now you are availing yourself of what we hope is a good and relevant book about your moving forward, from good to *great*, in your governance potential.

Thanks for all you do.

Thanks for being a Difference Maker!

✅ Difference-Making Tips

◆ Difference Makers ensure, when communicating with fellow board members and their superintendents, that all involved are able to look backward with pride in what they have contributed and forward with hope. In other words, Difference Makers take a few moments to value and affirm what others have said before moving on to what they say themselves.

◆ Difference Makers realize there are two kinds of community members: voters and future voters. Each community member they meet could someday vote to bring them onto the board or to take them off. Difference Makers recognize this while shopping or gassing up the car each week. Difference Makers especially realize this with those less fortunate in life circumstances than themselves.

◆ Difference Makers know that superintendents play a critical role in the board's finding common ground. In order to keep boards from becoming agenda/emotion focused, a superintendent must provide training, information, and education to the board. This helps boards make decisions based on data, facts, information—not someone's supermarket conversation or emotional experience. This also takes some heat off board members—they have evidence and justification for doing something or not doing something.

◆ Difference Makers realize that their governance is only as good as their next day's best work. This is particularly important because that "big win" they think they may get with immediate board action will be remembered much longer by them than anyone else around them. Even those for whom they are advocating will move on much more quickly to the "next issue." What this means is that so-called one-plank wonders (persons with narrow agendas desiring board election) will quickly realize that they do little good in terms of board service and that the little good they bring is soon forgotten.

3

How to Maximize Constituencies

One board member's thoughts . . .

At times when driving home after board meetings, I can't get metaphors out of my mind.

Most recently, I envisioned my school district as a network of airports, with my role as a board member to ensure air travel safety. Like the Federal Aviation Administration (FAA), my decisions have real consequences.

It sounds a bit strange, but it's like we have passengers purchasing tickets to travel from a place of "needing something" to a destination of "getting something."

And my job is safe travel.

After all, my colleagues and I authored the regulations. And we hired those who enforce them.

Superintendents are our air traffic controllers, ensuring that our planes chart intentional routes, avoid midflight collisions, and make safe landings. School employees manage our network of airports. A variety of folks serve as our pilots, ideally school principals, but even community power brokers—negatively or positively.

We try to keep the right people flying the planes, as passengers are stakeholders, including students, families, and community groups.

All traveling from where they are to a better place, hopefully.

Without all conditions optimal . . . planes could collide!

An interesting thing that I thought of recently is payment for the flight.

Whether a safe trip or not, the flying of planes takes investment. Costs are borne by passengers, even if the experience is not a good one.

As board members, we create conditions so that air traffic controllers, pilots, flight crews, and ground transportation can all work together safely, moving passengers from where they are in our schools to their intended destinations.

Note to self: Don't mess it up!

Resources in school districts are allocated in an opportunity/cost scenario. If one group gets something, that means there is less for everyone else.

Our constituents and even some board members may want to maximize what they "get." Unfortunately, this view can also mean that many times we need to work against others' efforts, both groups and individuals, because anything that they receive may mean that there is less for our favorite group or project.

Being able to accommodate best the needs of all students can be a challenge, but it is one that must always remain our focus.

Being able to accommodate best the needs of all students can be a challenge, but it is one that must always remain our focus. This work is accomplished through the involvement of constituencies.

A constituency in a school district has the following attributes:

1. Issues define it.
2. Power and influence are its tools.
3. People are involved.
4. Irrational people as well.

And . . .

5. A hierarchy of needs is always in play.
6. Those needs demand that a difference be made.

Constituencies are a fact of life for board members.

Balancing Constituencies' Expectations

Each constituency offers a gift of expectations.

Board members may have the band boosters constituency on one hand and the local business community (Chamber of Commerce) on the other. Let's not forget our local teachers unions and our special needs advocates, both championing the rights of children and their own interests in distinctly different ways.

The delightful and intriguing thing about constituencies is that each typically has a cause that its members believe in, and if you were only talking to that constituency separately, the cause that they are most concerned about makes sense.

In a trial, if we only hear the prosecution, the defendant always seems guilty. Conversely, if we only hear the defense witnesses, we are confident of an innocent verdict.

Here's our line of thinking on this: Where's the downside of putting more resources (time, talent, and treasure) into fine arts? Where's the downside of focusing more in our programs on cost containment? Conversely, where's the downside of compensating folks well for the professional jobs that they do?

A downside really doesn't exist if these desires for action and advocacy are taken separately, *and* we have the resources to support them.

But that's not reality.

One explanation for why groups become ingrained over time is that the only viewpoints considered in order to make decisions are viewpoints that mirror their own. It is challenging to ask that they see beyond their own reach, let alone ask them to move beyond what is comfortable or known to them.

Social media doesn't exactly help. If we hang around only like-minded folks in terms of the space in which we exist, not only do we believe we are correct more often than not, but we may not even realize that other points of view exist.

We have a huge blind spot.

This is not to indict the Internet or those who choose with whom they connect. It is simply a mention of the challenges that constituencies provide board members, as many do not comfortably exist in one another's alternative worlds. But they expect you as a board member to provide for them, in theirs. And believe us, these constituencies will know crystal clear and will remind you of what their worlds include, at times with little consideration of their limitations.

However, the clear and present fact is that, as a board member, you are a steward of community sentiment. A savior, in fact. Your superintendent should remind you aptly that only so much investment can take place and that pleasing one constituency within increasingly tight budgets will require an obligation to de-invest in another constituency's heartfelt needs (even if really only "wants"). Just about anything can be accomplished, but what is the cost to another initiative or program?

Over time, this can increase resistance to a school district's efforts, if board members are not out in front, tending to the needs of constituencies and providing an ever-present, listening ear. Each constituency thinks their "babies" are the cutest, and, by not cooing at them, you might give the impression that you think they're a bit homely.

It may be easy as a board member to remove yourself when it is a hypothetical situation and even chuckle at the silliness of those who seem to have selfish, small-picture viewpoints. What becomes more challenging is if we have to step back from causes that we personally believe in or that were part of a platform that we ran on when attempting to gain election or appointment to the board. And maybe even more difficult is if it is a cause our neighbors, friends, spouse, or children want us to fight for.

It is definitely easier as a pre–board member to have lots of ideas to improve the system. There is almost a honeymoon phase for a while immediately after being elected or appointed . . .

Until you discover there is a reason why your good idea won't or can't work.

Until you are educated on the budget limitations or regulations.

Until you understand legislative requirements and restrictions.

So many times, when considering a run or actually running for school board office, the candidate does not have all the information.

This can result in members, once elected, feeling frustrated, disenchanted, or even detached upon better understanding of what they just volunteered to do (or not do).

How do we remember to step back and make sure we focus on the needs of everyone rather than on our personal interests?

Additionally, what if some of our fellow board members seem to lack this skill and understanding of the proper responsibilities of a governing body?

Embracing Complication

In terms of your board member role with the constituencies who rely upon you, things are complicated.

To try to list all of the given constituencies that will greet you as a board member (and to provide a recipe for each) would not make sense here, as your community is undoubtedly different from those of others who are reading. We do attest, however, that anywhere you lead . . . anywhere you govern . . . anywhere you serve, a small number (at least) of constituencies will make their voices heard and these voices will invariably be contradictory. They won't often make great harmony together in song, to use a musical metaphor.

Probably as a board member, you are surrounded by the people who are like you or have similar interests. Therefore, often it seems that not only are there contradicting constituencies but also that they will probably be represented by different board members. While this is actually not bad, it creates interesting board interaction and discussion. Rarely will the vocal constituencies talk to *all* the board members. They will undoubtedly find one or two on the board—then make their case. This creates different perspectives and "solutions" for board members, and it can be complicated and taxing on relationships.

Board members who believe that their superintendents will be able to stave off their never-ending state of contradiction are probably a bit naïve and unrealistic.

Superintendents can't make it all go away.

And you shouldn't want them to.

You know different, as we live in a world where stability is only a fleeting respite from change, complication, and a bit of unpredictability. And, to be quite honest, stability is the calm before any given, next storm.

The saving grace is that, in most communities, there really is order in chaos.

Constituencies behave predictably.

You know this. You have lived with them for years, probably went to school with many of them, worked with them, worshiped with them, and socialized with them. You knew their parents. Possibly you have relatives who have married into their families.

People don't surprise you much because you're a good judge of "What's up?"

After all, you were elected on the shoulders of your own friends, colleagues, neighbors, and thus constituencies who wanted to turn feelings into action.

They did this by electing you!

Congrats for that! They needed something, and they had the confidence to give you the platform to make it happen on their behalf.

And rest assured, their interests will change, even if they don't realize it.

The key for you now is to realize what others may not: Your special role in governance involves more a marathon of policy-making obligation than a sprint of issues management.

The key for you now is to realize what others may not: Your special role in governance involves more a marathon of policy-making obligation than a sprint of issues management. It is actually humbling to think that, as board members, our actions can have reverberating effects upon our schools and upon hundreds if not thousands of children (and future adults) for lifetimes to come.

That's now what we must consider when listening to what our constituencies want and when determining what we can and should provide to them. Everything we provide has an intended effect, as well as unintended effects, that can last decades. This is where the power of your governing body can help.

Difference Makers understand that best practices in constituency communication include listening more and talking less, facilitating more and directing less, and stewarding more and managing less. We could listen more and talk less by verbally recapping what a community member has said and seeking confirmation that we got it correct, before offering an opinion of our own (and to use the word "and" more often than "but"). We could facilitate more and direct less by providing the telephone number of the superintendent or principal to concerned citizens and encouraging them to reach out, rather than saying, "I'll take care of that." We could steward more and manage less by tactfully letting friends and neighbors know that board action is taken as a group after thoughtful conversation, not as individuals playing "fix-it," issue by issue.

> **Difference Makers understand that best practices in constituency communication include listening more and talking less, facilitating more and directing less, and stewarding more and managing less.**

Sometimes board members do not even realize when they are practicing best practice and when they are not. Often, well-intentioned board members think they are being helpful and movers and shakers when, in actuality, they aren't always able to see why a lot of talking, fixing, and directing isn't a good long-term plan and how that can injure the integrity of themselves or their entire board.

In board meetings, our best boards of education function as their own "living constituency" where, even among myriad viewpoints, membership sees the bigger picture and thus coalesces, filtering and vetting options at its disposal, to arrive at a clear picture of community sentiment before making its decision on action items that are important to all.

They try to do the most good and offer the least amount that's not good. And they keep their eye on things larger than themselves and their friends. Each realizes, along the way toward "doing good," that he or she is only one member of a group in the decision making.

✓ Difference-Making Tips

♦ Difference Makers keep watch and listen for the next constituency with a need that is going unmet. This is best done in local shops, in stores, on walks, over neighborhood fences, and at the ball game. Getting involved locally in our own family's weekly schedule serves up prime opportunities to reach out and connect positively with those who depend on us.

♦ Difference Makers understand how to involve constituencies. They understand how to keep constituencies focused and how to keep them informed. This is through strategic planning and structured committee participation—in other words, getting them involved in areas that will allow them to see the bigger pie, not just one slice.

♦ Difference Makers practice stepping back to focus on the needs of everyone rather than their own personal interests by having breakfast or lunch with the board member who votes in opposition to them most often and by striving to listen more than they talk. And by picking up the bill.

♦ Difference Makers understand that, if fellow board members seem to lack big-picture decision making, they can help them achieve this skill by using personal anecdotes in work sessions of how they are struggling with embracing the big picture yet are still making decisions based upon it anyway. Over time, their testimony will serve as vicarious learning opportunities for those who need a lesson in moving beyond a narrow agenda.

♦ Difference Makers understand best practices in constituency communication include listening more and talking less, facilitating more and directing less, and stewarding more and managing less.

♦ Difference Makers ensure metaphorically that we as board members don't fly the airplanes. Our job is more about ensuring safe air travel and empowering and sustaining others who more rightfully have the controls for taking passengers (constituents) from a place of needing something to a place of getting something.

4

How to Communicate with and Manage Constituencies

One board member's thoughts . . .

It's hard to "turn it off."

Even at work during the day, I'm often approached regarding my other "me"—the 24/7 school board member.

I'll admit that board service is more like a calling than a job, more of a mission than a position. It's a labor of love, actually. I'd be hard-pressed to give it up.

The only problem is that I'm expected to have many relationships with constituents, all wanting fidelity, if not monogamy.

Note to self: Underpromise; overdeliver. Don't get into a relationship impulsively.

As we noted in our last chapter, a constituency in a school district has the following attributes:

1. Issues define it.
2. Power and influence are its tools.
3. People are involved.
4. Irrational people, as well.

And . . .

5. A hierarchy of needs is always in play.
6. Those needs demand that a difference be made!

Think of a group of folks who want to allow a scouting group to meet in the evenings and who want the school opened to them with custodians on hand and the lights and heat that you provide. On the surface, you hear their requests as reasonable, having to do with community engagement and making a positive difference for children. It is pretty hard to argue with these things, as they resonate with most of us. In fact, many of us harken back to our own involvement in scouting and what it did for us.

Might we suggest that a constituency is out there feeling differently?

What about those in a vengeful, local group that wants this or that to happen? What about the same bumper crop of malcontents who show up to every board meeting and pepper the board with negativity? What about those who perennially threaten board member recall elections?

First, it is important to understand and reflect: Why does this group feel so vengeful? Often the "issue" isn't really the issue—it just is manifesting itself there. Is there a lack of trust with the school system? Why might there be?

Let's dissect: This group—the constituency—has issues that define it. Power and influence are its tools. People are involved (some unpredictable at times), and it's now causing you trouble as a board member.

What to do?

The best part is next.

A Difference Maker like you knows that a hierarchy of needs is always in play and that those needs demand difference to be made.

Here's where you get an entry point with this group.

The group has a need to be heard, but more importantly, its individual members have a need to be heard. And some of these folks probably haven't been heard in quite some time, or, at minimum, they don't believe they have been listened to, which is equally relevant.

Can you use your difference-making ability to lend an ear not necessarily to the collective, vengeful whole but to the individual members who joined the ranks of this group for a reason: a need unmet?

Maybe one member has had a need for peace during breakfast each morning for the past five years instead of fighting with his children to go to school. Maybe another sees that school has become more disengaged from their children's interests and has made promises that things will get better, and doesn't know how to *make* it better. Maybe their hearts are breaking for things they regret that they have done to mess up their lives and those of their children. Maybe they are not very skillful in parenting, yet really want to be thought of as competent in the minds of their own children.

Maybe all they need is unconditional, positive regard. Quite possibly, a good first step would be to receive an affirmation from you—a board member.

These unmet needs might *not* be completely your school district's fault, certainly not your school board's fault, but they are people's needs nevertheless.

Oh, and another thing: Each constituency as a whole has a need too—it has the need *to meet* its membership's needs.

In short, it needs to make a difference.

Beyond their veneer, all constituencies are like insecure teenagers in terms of their basic needs. Board members like you, who understand this best, can make a difference.

How Difference Makers Serve

The best board members see the good and bad in constituencies for what they are yet promote the positive energy over and above their bad energy. They ensure that they pay positive and continual attention to those things that are helpful to the board and

> **The best board members see the good and bad in constituencies for what they are yet promote the positive energy over and above their bad energy.**

mutually agreeable among constituencies and less attention to those that cannibalize one another.

Exercising the good leg, not the bad, is the operational metaphor here.

If the scouting group and area fast-food lobby all share a common interest in helping the local humane society have a pet-friendly hiking trail on school grounds, that will be where the Difference Maker spends time and energy. It's not as important where you are placing your energy as a Difference Maker as that you *are* placing your energy in places where people can find common ground and that people are given adequate space in your life and in your ear. Your attention as a board member is really one of quality, not equality. Yet, as perceived, also one of quantity.

Providing unconditional, sustainable respect along with consistent affirmation is key!

Please be encouraged to use your superintendents in this regard as well.

Our best boards know that the superintendents they hire can and should work with community groups to provide for their individual members' needs for safety, love, and belonging. Use your superintendent, and expect your superintendent to work with the people—to connect and to affirm. Over time, with a superintendent properly deployed and with your kind and continuing ear as a board member, your constituencies will discern more often a common ground upon which to operate, and they can leverage these collaborative opportunities to address more positively the issues that provide for the identity of the constituency in the first place.

By establishing that we listen but respond neutrally to all requests sets a tone that we can do this when we receive negative requests. However, if we excitedly say "yes" to the Boy Scouts in a public meeting request, then we will have to respond similarly to a negative group who requests to use the facility. Instead, if we follow the procedures and share professionally with the Boy Scouts that they need to contact the proper school district employee with their desire, then we can do the same thing when we are approached by a less-desirable faction. However, if we want to be the good guy and assure the Boy Scouts they can use it, then we must be ready to be the bad guy when we tell someone else "no." Rather, we can always be professional by keeping decisions where they should be made rather than doling out favors when they are ones we want to grant.

This is especially important because perhaps the reason the problem may have started in the first place is due to a perception that the leadership (administration and/or board) doles out favors. Whether or not this is actually happening, the perception is out there.

How do good boards and superintendents protect themselves against such perceptions? By offering clear, accessible, and easy-to-understand procedures for requesting and granting access or services.

How does the board communicate proper procedure and process? By tactfully redirecting inquiries to the superintendent's Central Office, where they can find those clear, accessible, and easy-to-understand procedures for requesting and granting access or services.

How does the board communicate that there *are* procedures and policies? Through parent and community bulletins, in newsletters around town in waiting rooms and public areas, and, of course, by mentioning it thoughtfully in board meetings—and, of course, with a commitment to *follow* board policies.

How does the board educate the constituency? By first of all, being patient with community members who don't catch on too quickly and serving as good teachers of governance and stewardship with unconditional positive regard for those who elected them.

Difference Making at All Levels

The dreams of our constituents may change over time, but they do not disappear. As a board member, you have a pivotal role through relationships to encourage all those with whom you come in contact to feel significant through the difference you make in their lives. This difference is not made by offering continual assurances of short-term promises but by being genuine, approachable, and kind when community members are entrusting you with their passions and with the direction of their children's current and future education.

By practicing the skills of positive and deferential difference making on a regular basis, we are capable of employing them as a natural extension of our regular repertoire. We must not only model constituency mindfulness on a continual basis, but we must intentionally *want* to connect with constituencies, to find common ground among them, to encourage them away from short-term bursts of expectation and into longer-term initiatives that can live beyond us all.

> We must intentionally *want* to connect with constituencies, to find common ground among them, to encourage them away from short-term bursts of expectation and into longer-term relationships with initiatives that can live beyond us all.

As we do this, it makes not only our own board service more meaningful in terms of keeping friends long after our terms expire, in a practical sense, it makes the next referendum seem less daunting. It might be said for the future of our schools, we need *all* constituencies on board—with the board, typically.

Holding those with whom we live, work, and play in high regard, while exercising our governance, will allow for making a difference in their lives, all the while engendering heightened levels of deference and trust in our decisions made as local policymakers, as well as higher levels of satisfaction with and loyalty to our students, our schools, and ourselves.

✔ Difference-Making Tips

◆ Difference Makers attribute human characteristics to constituencies, and by doing so they are able to simplify their relationships with community groups and leverage resources to meet their needs. They use finesse to work with the underlying dimensions that influence the behavior of the constituency's members, rather than running around haphazardly after individuals.

♦ Difference Makers appreciate the diversity in constituencies and embrace the challenge that their desires oftentimes compete with one another. They also see the diversity in constituencies reflected through the diversity within their boards. Every board member feels the angst when they are called to "fight the good fight"; however, our best board members see finite resources as an opportunity to bring people together through critical conversation and an opportunity to, as Stephen Covey noted in his fifth habit, "Seek First to Understand, Then to Be Understood."

♦ Difference Makers weigh the merits of competing interests and help their superintendents prioritize needs among constituencies. They resist enabling and professionally redirect those bending their ears, applying pressure, and bullying the board into fixing problems that are better left for district and building leaders.

5

What Boards of Education Are Really About

One board member's thoughts . . .

A mentor once told me, "Don't worry about things you have control over because you have control over them." And also, "Don't worry about things you don't have control over because you don't really have any control over the outcome anyway."

What I didn't know at the time is how much control I could enjoy by choosing "not" to exercise immediate control over something, yet rather to influence the conditions through which control is assumed.

Note to self: Look beyond one's immediate impact, to something more meaningful and powerful.

Our best boards of education do not run school districts. And they shouldn't. Superintendents run school districts. Principals run schools. Teachers run classrooms. And parents run households. It's really not complicated. Our nation's best boards have the confidence and competence to keep this straight.

What boards of education are really about is providing the governance so that schools can be run in the first place. Governance

What boards of education are really about is providing the governance so that schools can be run in the first place. Governance and leadership are different. and leadership are different. Both are important, yet the board should be doing the former, and the superintendent the latter.

Let's tease this out a bit more.

The "Job" of a Board

The board of education has in most communities the authority to set the direction under which business occurs in its schools. We used an aviation metaphor prior; we'll take a nautical approach here. It's almost as if boards of education have the ability to draw the maps and conditions in which direction ships set sail. They design the prevailing winds, determine the water currents, and even include the landmasses that ships should either avoid or set port in. They even provide fuel for passage. This is akin to setting policy and budget, one might say. In optimal conditions, the building of the ship itself would be left to facilities management, and the navigation and sailing of the ship would be left to the superintendent and building principals.

To tease out this analogy further: Maps need to be read and clearly communicated to the navigator, as maps are very static and sometimes require minor adjustments and nuances depending on roadwork or unforeseen conditions. Boards are excellent places to serve as *advisers* when this happens.

Some boards of education experience a problem in which the wrong people want to be designing the maps. This would be when the superintendent wants to set the direction for everything—when someone wants the board to be a rubber stamp. In those instances, someone is usurping the governance authority or policy-making power of the board, and this does not result in anything good. In other cases, mapmakers want also to sail the ships, and this results in someone not duly licensed at the helm. This is when board members want to serve as school leaders. Not good as well.

And if we do not have all of this foundation developed correctly and if all the players do not know and operate in their roles successfully, then we will really be in trouble when unexpected storms strike. What this chapter offers, maritime metaphor now aside, is an optimal relationship between a board and superintendent that works in terms of the difference making needed for local school districts and those people they serve.

In the optimal sense, the board of education has a specifically delineated job description, in which they:

1. Hire, evaluate, and, when necessary, dismiss the district superintendent;
2. Set overall policy for the school district;
3. Act upon (or amend) and assist in establishing the proposed budget; and
4. Represent community perspective/sentiment.

And then they pretty much let the educators do what they do best.

Our best boards leave to their superintendents the job of leading and managing operationally. They resist the temptation to "run" schools. After all, when board members are running schools, a void is left in governance. When all are leading, no one is governing.

Not good.

When Board Members Micromanage

Across our nation, we see things happening differently, especially with the pressures upon schools from government officials, bureaucrats, and the media. We see at times boards getting involved in areas outside of their governance roles, and the result is typically mission creep and micromanagement through faction or individual initiative. While in most cases it is well-meaning, it simply does not work for the long term, even if short-term, perceived gains are accomplished.

Boards then run the risk of exacerbating the problems that the schools are being criticized for by tinkering where they shouldn't.

If this is occurring in your school system, the question you may be asking is, "Now what?"

Imagine how difficult it is as a board member if you see one of your colleagues trying to micromanage the superintendent or principals. Who is going to deal with it? Superintendents are hard-pressed, as board members vote on their employment contracts.

It is probably better for the board president to have a critical conversation with members who are tinkering, while at all times keeping one thing in mind: This person is behaving as such because he or she wants to make a difference. Being inescapably human is a by-product of board service, while wanting what's best for our children.

Issues can be emotional and close to the heart.

Our hearts sometimes don't see things clearly because . . . well, they're hearts.

When board members micromanage, however, we often see conversations avoided. We often see no one wanting to address the issue. And it becomes worse as the person becomes more comfortable in a nonfunctional role that everyone else is enabling. It's no wonder why no one wants to talk about an elephant in the room.

Because it's an elephant!

And it's getting in the way, literally.

Yet conversations to get board members back on the team mustn't be avoided but rather carried out with respect, authenticity, and empathy, so that the board keeps its own responsibility to protecting its long-term governance responsibilities and superintendents can lead.

At times, micromanagement happens because board members feel the pressure of constituencies. Folks want things fixed! And maybe the superintendent is not doing things fast enough for them. According to them.

When this happens, it would be ideal if board members would be willing to go back and provide their friends and neighbors with a lesson on good governance and the benefits of addressing problems at their source. Some might say that expecting a board member under pressure to explain logically a board's role to a group of emotional people is just plain silly. And that one can't ignore the delicacies of living in a community while trying to govern in it.

Yet members *do* need to explain to constituents what the board's role is or isn't and to explain what that constituent can do to affect the situation (chain of command). Of course, boards like to help. That's why they ran for office! Part of their job, we would contend, includes training, educating, and empowering constituents properly.

Ideally, *listening* to emotional constituents is the maintenance that is oftentimes needed and, beyond that, channeling constituents toward places where grievances can be redressed. That is critical and allows board members to return to the important work that the board is to be about.

Yet because it is naïve to assume that all board members can do these things when approached by concerned community members, we'd like to discuss another way—one that offers an ounce of prevention as well—to stave off many of these circumstances.

It involves the board simply doing the jobs that they were elected to do.

Board members will find that if they use their policy and budgetary authority properly, the resultant, positive governance provides the oversight that allows our superintendent to lead in a way that tends better to the needs of that constituency.

How?

By not distracting our superintendent with board meddling.

It's mind-boggling how much Central Office time can be consumed by micromanagement on the part of a board of education.

The superintendent, through leadership and sound management, can show the local community in all its complexity that, as board members, we hear our community and, more than that . . . we are listening. And that board members will hold their superintendent accountable, when the school district leadership is allowed to do what they need to do without micromanagement—thus allowing board members to remain high above direct problem solving and daily operations, where duly elected board members exercising good governance should be.

It's not overly complicated for Difference Makers to stay in their governance grooves, yet it requires a certain amount of resilience to ask community members to take their concerns to the right operational person (leader), so that more than a short-term "fix" can be provided.

Having said that, the board's only employee is the superintendent, to whom board member concerns should be addressed. When board members have concerns over district operations, they should not be jumping past the superintendent to his or her subordinates. Yet, for community concerns brought *to* the board, it is best for board members to refer constituents to the proper levels of the chain of command. Whether or not board members should give the superintendent a heads-up would depend on whether this is an isolated issue or one in which a pattern is developing. Of course, more serious issues should always involve a team huddle with Central Office.

> **The board's only employee is the superintendent, to whom board member concerns should be addressed.**

Doing so will produce an optimal relationship between Difference Makers on school boards and their superintendents.

Working Relationships: Individual Board Members and Superintendents

In order for Difference Makers to feel at home while resisting the temptation for quick fixes and direct involvement in management, an optimal relationship must be established early, as soon as the superintendent is hired. This is where everyone involved has one "win" (the hire) and no "losses" (issues that arise). It may be the last time the team is undefeated, so enjoy and capitalize on the moment, but it is certainly one where a winning season can be launched.

Board members can expect the best superintendents to keep them in the loop. As Difference Makers, you should always be connected individually, even if you're not in a position of board leadership. Your voice needs to be heard when concerns come your way that will help guide your superintendent in decision making. Expect that, from time to time, your superintendent will reach out to you proactively to hear what is on your mind. If you find you need to make a call yourself, please be tactful in how many times you do.

Whether it is over morning coffee and breakfast prior to your workday or via sidebar at the dance recital, it is critical that you and your superintendent find quality and reasonable time to connect and work on your individual, one-on-one relationship. Great superintendents will take the preponderance of responsibility for making this happen at your convenience.

> **It is critical that you and your superintendent find quality and reasonable time to connect and work on your individual, one-on-one relationship.**

During these opportunities, hopefully your superintendent will be doing more of the listening than the talking. After all, you are the one offering community sentiment; you are articulating the passions of certain constituencies, and that is an efficient and effective use of the limited time you have.

Please know that if the shift in conversation occurs where you want something taken care of right away, you may be veering from your governance role; so be patient when the superintendent gently redirects your urgency with a need to explore further and make a decision that takes all factors into account. This may be difficult, but it's important for you to develop this resilience.

In short, the fewer direct promises you make to your local community members who approach you, while showing that you care for their viewpoints, the more comfortable you will be in your governance role and the more you will be comfortable staying away from micromanagement.

Always remember that we want to tell the Boy Scouts "yes" but then we might want to tell the other group "no." Yet other board members may want to tell the Boy Scouts "no" and the other group "yes." And in other cases, if we tell the Boy Scouts "yes," we might be legally obligated to say "yes" to other groups that we deplore. So rather than any of us getting caught in this web and minimizing board integrity and purpose, we need to make sure that all of us, in advance, agree to let the appropriate district employees deal with both groups and all groups.

Over time, this will reap big dividends, as your individual relationship with the superintendent will grow in terms of trust and aligned interests, and, believe it, the quicker things will happen when you want them to happen. And let's not forget that many districts have lost good superintendents due to micromanaging and find out that the grass is not necessarily greener with the next arrival.

✔ Difference-Making Tips

♦ Difference Makers clearly articulate an optimal board/ superintendent relationship in terms of the board (the *what* of policy) and the superintendent (the *how* of operation).

♦ Difference Makers run mostly marathons in their governance and not so many sprints. They are more about the long term than the short term. Board members who demand quick action are oftentimes those who have an inability to conceive of larger issues or think more deeply about the indirect consequences of immediate actions.

♦ Difference Makers recognize that although they run more marathons than sprints, they need training for both— how to run the marathon and what to do if a starter gun goes off in a sprint. Action can happen in both, but it is definitely *different* action. Especially critical is understanding what *is* appropriate action and why. Sometimes the action is policy-making and advising; at other times, the action is listening and channeling chain of command (marathons and mid-distance racing). Rarely, crises occur (sprints). All are important in heading for the "win."

♦ Difference Makers are those who rise above the fray. They do not vote along faction lines and are not quid pro quo in their behavior. They refrain from bickering and do not find backstabbing fashionable. They are the type of adults you wish your children would be when they grow up.

6

How Boards Can Govern More Effectively

One board member's thoughts . . .

I can't believe one of my colleagues is on the board.

Sometimes, I think that he is serving vicariously to "right some indiscernible wrong" that probably happened 20 years ago while he was in school.

And now through his children, sadly.

The biggest problem is that I don't believe he sees what other board members see in him: an adult seemingly as dysfunctional as the groups he will not stop editorializing about.

I hope he finds peace and another outlet for his service.

Note to self: Don't be THAT *guy.*

Under typical state statutes, board members are limited in authority to act and do what they do when they meet as a group. Individually, board members are not "on the clock" in terms of their power and authority. We have seen and heard of board members in some locales visiting buildings and telling principals and teachers what to do, heaven forbid determining which coaches will be fired.

If this has been something you have witnessed, we encourage you to "Just say *no!*"

We hope that not a lot of you out there have found yourself in those circumstances, but they are more common than we would like to admit.

And—for all their good intentions—people want to make a difference, and that's what they know how to do.

Sometimes, they just don't know how to go about it the right way, or they have emotional issues that they are bringing into their local service.

In any event, the point is that true Difference Makers wouldn't act like this, even if they did have the power under state law, which in most cases they don't. Difference Makers know that decisions through board consensus are more likely to be enacted by leadership with the tools to implement them directly and that those decisions are longer-lasting in terms of the difference they can make.

To be honest, we have found when the board of education hires a superintendent who is taking care of things operationally, then the temptation to micromanage has little need to rear its ugly head.

That's why we suggest building upon the wins of that undefeated team at the point of hiring, which guarantees a continued winning record and thus creates a more positive leadership team morale.

One thing presented in the later chapters of this book has to do with the professional development that a superintendent organizes for board members. In addition to asking their boards to spend their time learning something collaboratively, superintendents should always use a portion of that time to attend as learners themselves. This can serve to build a collaborative, colearning relationship between board members and superintendents, as collective Difference Makers. It's also good role modeling for the rest of the school district because it shows that the board is a professional group. It shows that the board expects employees to be up-to-date in best practice, and it shows that the board is informed and knowledgeable.

In summary, the best model for school board and thus for school district governance is when boards of education hire, evaluate, and at times dismiss their superintendents, set policies and budgets, reflect and pass along community sentiment, and then, with all due respect, step aside from direct school operations and let the educators do what they do best—promote children's learning.

And, yes, an occasional sidebar with the superintendent about the concerns or worries of *this group or that* is helpful for board members to pass along, though they are much better shared in a doughnut shop at 6 a.m. than through a board member's filibuster at a public board meeting.

When this happens, it demonstrates that a school district's governance is not one of difference making and is more reflective of "me" than "we" . . . or "our children."

This also sheds light on the small size of a pond and a fish's need to appear big.

Not fashionable.

How Difference Making Looks Out for You

Doing the right thing is in *your* best interest and an essential element to your board leadership and difference making. Doing the right things from the start means not spending your valuable time as board members dealing with trivial details because that is someone else's job—the superintendent's, for starters.

> **Doing the right things from the start means not spending your valuable time as board members dealing with trivial details because that is someone else's job—the superintendent's, for starters.**

For example, you will all receive a call from angry constituents, most likely parents. And *yes*, lending a kind ear is the thing to do, but please don't think it is in your best interest to take up your valuable time resolving it or, heaven forbid, promising a resolution. Maybe these parents have half the facts. Maybe what they want will actually work against them rather than for them, yet they are simply too close to the issue to realize it.

When constituents call you with concerns, please listen to them with respect. You will undoubtedly want to build into your schedules double the time in any given weekend's shopping trip so that you can exercise your community listening skills around every new aisle. This is natural for board members to experience.

Yet we also suggest that you never make a promise to those aggrieved, except, of course, the promise that you will give them leadership's telephone number for the direct sharing of their concern.

There are some instances where we realize that it is incredibly tempting for you to *want* to fix the problem that you are hearing about, either because (1) the person is 100% *right* or (2) the person is tapping into a *passion* that *you* have.

You might even feel that you will be a hero if you can resolve it.

And you might be!

Yet, please be careful, in that while in this instance the problem may be something you are deeply invested in—perhaps the assistant principal who picked on your own child—we implore you to handle it with the same compassion, redirection, and *distance* that you would all other issues because the next grocery store sidebar might be about the chess club tryouts, dance team cuts, or National Honor Society induction, and you might not want to go anywhere near those!

Please understand as a Difference Maker that whatever infantry-level action you take personally or how "low" you embrace as your role on the organizational food chain, *this level of action* becomes the new bar at which you will be pressured to address *all* future complaints (or reap push-back).

If you react to some issues extravagantly and others not, it looks like you have an agenda, are not interested in the whole, or unresponsive. None of these items are attractive qualities in a board member/representative.

You become a target.

In other words, if you decide to try to have a student's two-day suspension from school or a Friday football game suspension overturned, you might as well sign up to be the actual assistant principal or athletic director. And get ready because we know that from time to time, these positions will be on the chopping block, and so will yours at the next board election. That is because you will, from that point forward, be expected to make uncomfortable *win/loss* decisions for children on a regular basis that will have a negative long-term result for you.

Your difference making will be cut off at the knees.

You've just taken up a new version of Whac-A-Mole.

Additionally, what if you want to revoke a suspension you think is unreasonable, you tell the person you plan on doing that, and it turns out this has been the practice for years. Are you going to undo all of the previous suspensions?

Even worse, what if your niece is involved?

In this situation, even if you are right, you will be perceived as wrong by the community. It is much better to establish in advance how the board and administration will deal with things and then stick to this plan, even when it is personal.

Actually, you'll want to stick to it, *especially* when it is personal.

First, this takes pressure off of you, preserves your relationship with community, and showcases the *process* to the community. Boards and superintendents should not operate on whims, emotionally. Our best boards and superintendents are calm, structured, and thoughtful—anticipating problems before they happen, proactive and not reactive. So it's much easier to address emotional issues when guardrails have been put in place; it's less personal when solutions come out of a process or policy than when they seem arbitrary.

These difficulties, as you know, tend to present themselves when you're sitting in a formal board of education meeting, as you'll undoubtedly be put in a position during public commentary to hear parental or community complaints. You'll see that your colleagues on the board who have more the tendency to offer personal commentary (or even a grimace or eye roll) will reap a bad hand dealt in the future, even from other board members who will distance themselves from them.

The cardinal mistake would be saying, "We'll take care of this for you!" when a parent shares a story of woe or misery. Be careful of a snake, albeit charming, ready to bite. Once you get into the morass of "taking care of things," you will be expected to do the same for all comers—and have little or no time left for the business of school governance.

One question on your mind might be, "Well then, how *do* board members listen when addressed in a meeting?" After all, it is such an awkward time. The media is there and the community as well. The reality is that the worst thing boards can do is say, "We'll fix it," but it is also important to acknowledge the sharing and show that the board has listened. How does a good board do this well?

Typically, the following things work:

1. Having the board president *thank* the community member for bringing this concern to the board's attention and then paraphrase back to the community member the issue they have verbalized;

2. Ensuring that *only* the board president responds at that point;

3. Having other board members taking notes on what the person is saying with a serious look, yet not projecting too much emotion nonverbally in terms of either support, agreement, or disagreement. Unconditional positive regard and respectful attentiveness should be projected, as that person's voice should be heard and understood by all on the board;

4. Then, having the board president turn to the superintendent, who will then serve as the clarifier and contextualizer, noting the process that will take place in looking into the community member's concern and a timeline for when the community member might expect a response or additional information from the superintendent or appropriate school officials.

Superintendents should protect the difference-making function of their boards of education. This is especially important because if board members mishandle issues of community import even once, they will assuredly deal with anger and unhappiness as future decisions come their way. Board members need to stay out of the direct theater of operations because they are private citizens trying their best to live their lives and run their businesses.

They need to be protected to make a difference.

The Proper Power Dynamic

A helpful conceptual depiction of a school district's power and responsibility dynamic is depicted when three very important entities—superintendent, the board as a whole, and the board president—create a positive, symbiotic relationship so that difference making results (Donlan & Gruenert, 2016). Helping maintain the symbiotic relationship includes trust, deference, assurance, and humility.

In an ideal sense:

1. Superintendents **trust** their boards to reflect what the community wants of their schools; boards trust superintendents to do "just that." Boards trust that board Presidents and superintendents communicate frequently so that issues are handled and no surprises result (Donlan & Gruenert, 2016).
2. Boards offer **deference** to superintendents for leadership and operations; superintendents defer policy-making to boards. They then operate with loyalty under the policies drafted (Donlan & Gruenert, 2016).
3. Board presidents provide **assurances** to superintendents that they can lead without micromanagement; superintendents provide assurances to board presidents that they are open to questions and inquiries. Board members provide assurances that they will not use individual status operationally (Donlan & Gruenert, 2016).
4. Everyone understands the need for **humility** in mutual support as key to working relations. Board members understand that they do not have the specialized skills of superintendents, and superintendents understand that board members best know their communities (Donlan & Gruenert, 2016).

Boards that spend time on minutiae are abrogating their responsibilities of governance. This reminds us as authors of what we heard once about time spent in decision making as we ascended in our own educational careers. Teachers must respond in the moment. Assistant principals have a bit of time for some investigation. Principals can schedule a meeting to consider a proper course of action, and superintendents can be deliberate in gauging the will of constituencies before moving forward.

Board members in their roles of governance have even more time.

Board members should first encourage constituencies to address their concerns at the proper place in the organization— that place is closest to the problem, with the persons directly involved. Oftentimes, this redirection reduces the angst, and much of the problem simply goes away. It also allows board members to spend time more on the larger issues, such as:

- ◆ Policy changes;
- ◆ Curricular adoptions;
- ◆ Staffing decisions;
- ◆ Purchasing;
- ◆ Infrastructure and facilities;
- ◆ Legal issues.

These issues are closer to the 10,000-foot level, have longer-lasting implications, and really do demand a prioritization of the board's time and attention. They affect literally thousands of persons or more, not just a small, vocal group.

Shortly after election, board members realize the heavy responsibilities placed on their time and talent. It is thus necessary for superintendents to help provide alternatives to your own energy spent in handling your community's other concerns—those *very real* to individual persons but *light* compared to the issues that are now privy "only" to your attention, those demanding longer-term attention that your positional stature requires.

This brings up a related point, as you are having meetings of your boards of education. Oftentimes, superintendents wish to have building administrators available during community remarks.

This is dangerous.

Pot shots can become the rule rather than the exception.

And it's typically because superintendents want some cover.

This can be awkward as well for board members who are trying to be Difference Makers. In these circumstances, board members may be asked to respond immediately to accusations levied.

Or they are left uncomfortably to look at those in the administration who are being maligned with press pool reporters in the room. This puts Difference Makers on the line, without much time to respond. Legal complications can even arise.

We suggest that board presidents excuse all building administrators except the superintendents from board meetings by the time the community comments and participation section is handled.

In such a venue, the board president or superintendent can then say to any concerned group, "This can be looked into by the principal." This more effectively acknowledges concerns and suggests that aggrieved persons can more appropriately meet privately with school officials to look into the issues involved.

Only weaker superintendents allow leadership team members or employees to get horsewhipped, so that they themselves are insulated. That is not what effective leaders do, and Difference Makers on school boards need to protect superintendents and leadership teams in that regard through the way board business is conducted. And by having appropriate expectations of those present.

Board meetings are held to conduct the business of the school district. They are not town hall meetings. Paying taxes does not give the right to people to say all that they want to say at a board meeting in the way that they want to say it. And no one is guaranteed satisfaction just because they send their children to your school district. Life just doesn't work that way.

> **Board meetings are held to conduct the business of the school district. They are not town hall meetings.**

Difference Makers know that if the school telephone is ringing at 8:00 a.m. the next day after a board meeting, then the issue that arose is probably important enough to last through an evening of reflection. If your superintendent or principals never hear from the folks who complain again, that is also a sign of whether or not it would have been worth your time to discuss it further in public.

As with many negative persons who toggle from issue to issue quickly, if we can encourage them to revisit the issue at a later time, let's say a few hours or days, they will often have moved on to something else, in another neighborhood or even community. This is true even when concerned citizens contact you as board members.

If you respond and ask them to offer a few dates and times that you could meet them for coffee and conversation, you'll probably find that only the more serious (and levelheaded) follow through with taking a bit more of their time to have a candid conversation, which is a great tactic for weeding out who really wants to work toward a resolution and who just wants to fire off a scud missile.

Spending time wisely and productively at board meetings cannot be overstated, as that is when board members have the power to govern and that is what the public needs them to do, even when the public doesn't realize it.

✅ Difference-Making Tips

♦ Difference Makers have critical conversations with their superintendents and teach others the advantages they can accrue from not making quick assurances or knee-jerk promises when concerned people get in touch with them. They understand well the problems that meddling in operations will cause them personally and how superintendents would better "have their backs" through handling those situations themselves.

♦ Difference Makers protect their leadership team members from blindsiding and potshots at board meetings by ensuring that meetings of the board do not degenerate into dysfunctional town hall meetings. This protects all parties and helps board members make a difference.

♦ Difference Makers do not attend board meetings for the benefit of their own egos. They contribute to making a school district a better place through wise contributions and sound decision making. They are there for the right reasons and do not grandstand.

Reference

Donlan, R., & Gruenert, S. (2016). *Minds Unleashed: How Principals Can Lead the Right-Brained Way*. Lanham, MD: Rowman & Littlefield.

7

The Superintendent as Your Shield

One board member's thoughts . . .

It's nice every once in a while to know that someone has my back when the tough decisions need to be made. And someone confident enough to deliver a message to my friends and neighbors that I don't want to deliver.

And to take full responsibility!

Oh, and by the way, someone is getting paid a pretty good salary to do it.

Note to self: Good superintendents provide "cover" and SHOULD.

As a school board member, you should be commended for the courage to put yourself out there continually in a way that exposes you to conversation, critique, and commentary. Your neighbors, clients, and families see you now in a role that they didn't prior to your election or appointment. It seems that everyone who has *attended* a school system thinks she or he knows how best to run one; this is almost as logical as thinking just because we all used the restroom this morning, we're qualified to be plumbers.

We have said before that this may be one of the biggest reasons that the most common businesses to open are restaurants: Everyone has been in one, so they think they know how to run one.

It can't be hard, can it?

Of course, restaurants are also the most common businesses to close. This is why, as board members, you need a bit of cover from the superintendent.

The superintendent is your *shield*.

Or at least should be.

If you don't believe everything you hear from us about board governance, please be encouraged to *believe that*.

Believe the *shield* is a must in your governance and stewardship.

Here's why.

You're approached daily or weekly by people wanting to know what is going on in our schools, and, by virtue of our plumbing metaphor, they think they know how to fix things.

Or they think you can! And should.

The problem is that even if you were to agree with what they were saying and try to help them further their aims 50% of the time, you would probably get what you both want only a certain portion of that. Meanwhile, you have upset about 50% of everyone you know by not acting on their behalf, and for a good portion of those you align with, you will appear powerless to them each time things don't go your way.

Ouch.

Who signed up for that?!?

Over time, this can chip away at the veneer of any positive community relationship and *your* reputation.

That's not what you signed up for.

You signed up to make a positive difference for children and possibly to increase your political stature in the process (not a bad thing), not to alienate yourself or become fodder for the banter of social media.

You signed up to make a positive difference for children and possibly to increase your political stature in the process (not a bad thing), not to alienate yourself or become fodder for the banter of social media.

Enter one with cape and superpowers, coming to save the day . . .

The *shield*!

Your superintendent.

In a private meeting with your superintendent regarding community upheaval over the varsity basketball program and lead coach, this might be said:

Board Member:	First, thanks for scheduling a board hearing on the situation with our varsity basketball coach, in the wake of the parent group's call for his resignation. It's no secret they have already identified a replacement once you fire the guy, and the difficult part is that my wife's cousin has been nominated by the group's spokesperson, my father-in-law. "So, no matter what I think of this whole darned situation, it's complicated. An interesting Sunday dinner this past weekend, as you can imagine."
Superintendent (Shield):	Hey, I get it. It's complicated for sure. What I do understand is that everyone involved here wants what's best for students, and we're all concerned our students get a chance to compete. Yet the administration's seeing things a bit differently than the parent group and possibly even a board member or two, which can be a bit awkward, especially in a close-knit community with family involved.
Board Member:	Any chance we could turn this into a win/win? I'm not sure the board is prepared to take all the heat.
Superintendent:	Certainly. I can draw the heat away from the board, as I don't want you all in a dicey position. You all have bigger things to worry about.
Board Member:	What do you suggest?
Superintendent:	To be honest, this is where I need to take some arrows that are being slung. I need to be your *shield*. Here's how.

I'm going to profess publicly that as this is a personnel issue, we can't really talk public about it just yet. Further, the board is not really involved directly at this point, and thus I must accept full responsibility for what is currently occurring. To explain further . . . if we *do* get into a position where there is a vacancy in our coaching ranks, then I'll need to bring candidates to you as a board for hire. But as of yet, we don't have a vacancy. As of right now, nobody has been removed.

And I'm not going to fire any coaches midseason. That wouldn't be fair to the student athletes who have become accustomed to a system, optimal or not. And regarding that, knowing where the group stood on playing time expectations for our boys this season over last, I had the athletic director pull together some data on this season's stats on playtime equity. You know what I found out?

Board Member: What?

Superintendent: I found out that all kids who attended regularly scheduled practices this season, and those with pre-excused absences, have not only played consistently in each game, I found that other players outside the starting five are actually playing much more than they did last year. The evaluation by the athletic director last year did what it was intended to do. The coach has followed her suggestions, and in doing so, he has built capacity. We may have our first winning divisional in 12 years.

Board Member: That's incredible. But the parents are not seeing this that way. The coach is not

	communicating. Would you be willing to share, and to field any criticism that remains?
Superintendent:	Not only that, but I'll share that the coach's evaluation this year, and next if he continues, will also have a goal to increase such communication directly to parents. I'll even share with the parent group your particular efforts, as well as others on the board, to hold *me* accountable for this issue as you have in closed session, and the fact that the voices of parents were heard, loud and clear. Finally, I'll share that if you're not all convinced that I'm doing the right thing, I'll accept responsibility in my *own* evaluation by the board.
Board Member:	Sounds fair, as long as you keep sharing all the facts and parents understand this information sooner, rather than later. Perception is reality.
Superintendent:	Of course I will. And I say that as well, because I'm especially watchful that someone with a personal vendetta against our coach, doesn't turn into someone else next time who has a personal vendetta against *you* or any board members. What about someone with a personal vendetta against your daughter, the junior varsity swimming coach? Wouldn't you want me protecting her in the same way as I have protected this coach, you, and all others I serve?
Board Member:	Your having our backs *first* is appreciated, as long as you have our students' backs *most*.
Superintendent:	I wouldn't have it any other way.

The challenge is continually understanding that, as board members, we have to have consistency in how we govern in spite of the community pressures we face.

The challenge is continually understanding that, as board members, we have to have consistency in how we govern in spite of the community pressures we face. By keeping in mind that *shields* are necessary to protect us as visionary leaders and by expecting those roles in our superintendents, we can elevate ourselves from dealing with the minutiae that interrupt our own personal and professional lives.

✔ Difference-Making Tips

◆ Difference Makers actively govern with a goal to manage positive relationships at all levels of their organization and community so that people tell them things in confidence. That way, they know what arrows might be launched against others and even themselves, so that they can alert their superintendents, who can deploy their *shields,* keeping policy-making protected and everyone above the fray.

◆ Difference Makers do not run frantically from constituent to constituent with little shields, promising to save every community member every time they are about ready to step out in traffic. Instead, the trick is to encourage their superintendents to use their shields judiciously to leverage the more important policy outcomes that they wish to achieve, not simply to handle every bit of operational "incoming" that seems urgent at the time.

◆ Difference Makers do not conceive of the superintendent-as-shield as a relationship of quid pro quo. They see it as necessary and natural in providing for sound governance and to keep the lines open for community conversation and input.

8

The Care and Feeding of Community Members

One board member's thoughts . . .

For quite some time, I thought that frank candor and authenticity were the best way to long-standing, positive relationships.

Then, after a few years on the board, I realized that while this was probably true in ideal circumstances, strategic relationship building worked better in real life.

Note to self: Not all "manufacturing" jobs are blue collar, especially those that create relationships.

Board members are in a unique situation in that they are generally elected by the public at large to govern school districts, yet in those roles they also serve as mentors and information providers to the community members they serve. This is because the board accumulates an inside track on how the school system is "really" run, given myriad issues that they experience as a governing body.

Community members, conversely, can only rely upon their own firsthand impressions of school or that of their children and families. They don't get the inside track or the depth of information that the board is provided.

And it is incumbent upon the board to provide for the proper care and feeding of those who elect them to their positions of governance and authority in the first place. Difference-making boards do this very well, indeed, and our smartest board members know how to do so without thinking too hard about it. Yet their minds are always wrapped around it.

Care of Community Members

Board members provide for the care of their community members, quite aptly, by considering their lower-order needs before providing for their higher-order needs. Abraham Maslow was the first and arguably the best in discussing a hierarchy of needs that must be met for human beings to live their lives productively and to function appropriately. In Maslow's hierarchy, lower-order needs take priority and provide the building blocks for one's meeting higher-order needs. The needs hierarchy starts first at the basic level of physiological needs, then moves upward through those pertaining to safety and security, next toward needs of love and belonging, then toward those involving self-esteem and even self-actualization. Visually, Maslow's hierarchy is denoted below:

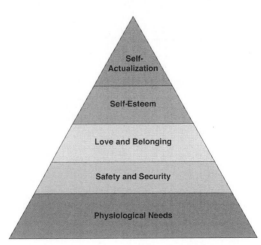

FIGURE 8.1 Visual Depiction of Abraham Maslow's Hierarchy of Needs

Source: Originally published in Maslow, A. (1043). A Theory of Human Motivation. Psychological Review, 50(4), 370–396.

In recent years, new and updated needs have been included amid and atop Maslow's model (cognitive, aesthetic, transcendence needs), yet for the sake of our discussion, Maslow's original hierarchy is just fine.

With respect to needs pertaining to safety and security, Difference Makers ensure that they provide a safe and orderly school system for community members and families. This ensures that they pay particular attention to emergency management policies, school building code issues, bullying prevention, and a host of other items that need the attention of governance each year.

Difference Makers know what policy decisions will tend to safety needs for their constituents, and they must be most careful to listen to what worries and fears lie at the heart of community sentiment. In one community, it might be proactivity in keeping convicted felons away from schools by opposing the half-way house project that a developer wants to bring to the neighborhood. In another, it might be an issue of whether or not it is safe to run multigrade sports teams. Difference Makers know what is "safe" in their communities and what is "unsafe" as well, given contemporary community sentiment *and* past experience.

The challenge at times, yet very important, is to balance community sentiment with the safety of students. Often these two pieces are aligned but sometimes not. Members are advocates not only for our community but also for people within our buildings. There must be conscientious balance and broad view of both. Hopefully, one is not at the expense of the other.

Board members provide for the care of their community by anticipating what "could" happen, given different courses of action, even if their community members do not anticipate it. This is what "care" of community is all about. The simple way to think of it is to be proactive rather than reactive—trying to anticipate what is needed rather than being vulnerable to hindsight 20/20 thinking.

Feeding of Community Members

By "feeding," we don't really mean feeding. Not with food anyway. Rather, effective Difference Makers work diligently to provide sustenance to community members in the areas of love, belonging, and self-esteem. Community members reach out to board members out of an authentic desire to get something that is good for their own children. At least, most of the time, they do. It only makes sense that board members would respond by affirming their personhood or convictions, valuing their input, and, hopefully in many instances, inviting community members to feel better about having had a conversation after it was complete rather than before it happened in the first place.

When differences are being made, the natural by-products are love, belonging, and a resultant, positive self-esteem in all involved.

Areas that offer potential for board members to connect with their constituents' needs for love and belonging include providing those who elect them a sense of collegiality and meaningful board connection. Difference Makers know how valuable it is to intentionally design situations in which community members can feel as though they matter to board members, professionally and personally, as those with family connections to school operations.

Difference Makers greet community members warmly when they are seen shopping or when they arrive at board meetings for public comment, even when issues are challenging to talk about. This is what love is all about. Community members want to "matter" to board members when they call with concerns or when they ask for consideration of a problem.

Community members want to "matter" to board members when they call with concerns or when they ask for consideration of a problem. Our best Difference Makers ensure it.

Our best Difference Makers ensure it.

Community members feel as though they belong when they are recognized by the board president at an open board meeting for their contributions of time, talent, and treasure they have put in working the football games, serving concession stand refreshments, volunteering at the elementary school library, or helping chaperone the trip to the big city museum for the 5th-grade class.

Board members might also check on how their schools connect positively with people "in little ways." Difference Makers know enough about their community members to know what makes them feel at ease, comfortable, and even right at home. Yes, Difference Makers ensure love and belonging.

Difference Makers also enhance their community members' self-esteem. Self-esteem includes one's own confidence, a sense of achievement, and perceptions of respect from others and of being valued. Difference Makers know how important these things are for community members. They make notes of the different constituency or parental groups in their communities and work with the board president to come up with a schedule of public recognition during the school year. They ensure affirmations of particular community members who are both respected and connected, so that these persons report positively to others that their contribution was appreciated.

Difference Makers ensure that community members hear what great things other community members have been doing in terms of their commitment to the district and accomplishments of the children. This allows, as Robert Frost once noted, for all to look backward with pride and forward with hope (even though, in reality, Frost was not writing about boards and their communities but rather about a dead old guy on a farm—yet we digress).

> Difference Makers ensure that community members hear what great things other community members have been doing, in terms of their commitment to the district and accomplishments of the children.

In short, receiving affirmation from others builds self-esteem.

A critical by-product having to do with community members' self-esteem is that of their self-efficacy. Self-efficacy is the personal belief that one is able to make a positive impact in one's own life through hard work and effort. Members of the public who have healthy self-efficacy tend not to be insecure; they are thus able to avoid conspiracy theories and typically do not do as much ranting about the "have's" and "have not's" on social media, for one thing. With self-efficacy, community members have a healthy sense of personal and interpersonal autonomy and behave rationally, while others around them may not.

Difference-making board members know that the path toward fostering self-efficacy in the public may very well travel through self-esteem, in that one might need to feel good before believing that one is capable, talented, and empowered.

Difference Makers teach and expect that all in the school district will thank and acknowledge members of the community through care and feeding. They serve as role models, mindful of Maslow's hierarchy. They are respectful diplomats while at the grocery store, gas station, barber, or coffee shop. They govern with an intent that their positive persona and mindful role modeling will help leaders, faculty members, and staff members make differences in their areas of responsibility as well.

Not only does this help with positive community relations, it also teaches others how to build effective relationships in their lives.

Care and feeding, while providing for others' needs, may seem like concepts that should inherently be understood by those elected to public office and, well . . . probably should. But if we don't take time to discuss what might seem to be basic expectations among all of us as friends and colleagues when times are good, we may find ourselves wishing that we had when times are bad.

Community members are really no different from us as board members, as we have all experienced both the opportunities and the need for care and feeding in our lives.

✔ Difference-Making Tips

◆ Difference Makers ensure a balance in their community member relationships. Like the best of parents, they do not want to be too distant, or the relationship doesn't grow positively. Yet they do not want to be too close, either, through the making of promises, or community members will take advantage of them.

- Difference Makers know how to have discussions with community members that do not directly mention "them" (community members) but that are really about them. They might say, "Imagine if . . ." so that the community members make the connection themselves with a bit of distance to reflect safely with self-worth.
- Difference Makers share with other board members what community members need in terms of care and feeding and what they need for themselves. Yet this requires some savviness of board members in order to determine what needs to be cared and fed or why, as overfeeding is not healthy and not all concerns arise from a lack of nourishment. Forgetting this could be a slippery slope on the way to ignoring the elephant in the room!
- Difference Makers know that the care and feeding of community members is much like making "bank deposits," knowing that eventually "withdrawals" will be needed. Those include situations when unpopular decisions have to be made, such as closing schools, consolidation, and the like. As there is really no up-side to these decisions (except longer-term fiscal solvency, of course), it pays to have more in the "relationship account" than one needs in terms of the necessary "withdrawal." At least you end up with a small balance with which to move forward.

Reference

Donlan, R., & Whitaker, T. (2017). *The Hero Maker: How Superintendents Can Get their School Boards to Do the Right Thing* (Eye On Education). New York: Routledge.

9

Holding Board Meetings

One board member's thoughts . . .

I once had a mug in my office that said, "Meetings Suck."

Believing that for a time, I then enjoyed a series of promotions, and the result was that I began to attend more and more meetings.

Over time, I have realized that meetings don't necessarily have to be that bad, but the people running them often are idiots.

They can parlay a five-minute conversation into a three-hour yawn fest.

Note to self: "Do" meetings the right way.

Board meetings are public, open meetings held to conduct the business of a school district. Contrary to the popular belief of some in local communities, board meetings are not town hall meetings. They are not intended to be meetings where the public arrives to demand actions and operational decisions better left to superintendents, principals, teachers, and staff members.

Rather, board meetings are ideally venues where groups of difference-making policy-makers come together to provide governance, thoughts, and direction on whether a school district is operating within guidelines established by board policy, whether the budget is sound, and whether the superintendent is acting effectively as the school district's CEO and/or COO (chief operating officer).

Our best Difference Makers understand that in myriad locales and circumstances, the only time board members have legitimate governing authority is when a quorum is held at a public meeting, as per the board's bylaws or state law. That is when the board can rightfully act to conduct business.

Outside of regularly held work sessions and board meetings, most board members have no greater authority than do regular community members. If community members individually would not have authority to make demands upon school officials, then board members really shouldn't be doing it either.

Regrettably, it has been witnessed in certain locales that rogue board members feel they can arrive at school buildings, any time they wish, and tell principals or teachers what to do. They wander around and stir up trouble. Getting teachers to fill out a petition of "No confidence for the superintendent" has happened more than once. Showing up to use the wood shop to use tools or opening the gym for their child to practice shooting baskets might happen from time to time. There are even instances when board members will want to accompany the drug dogs on a search of school lockers for contraband, of all things!

The point we're trying to make, which true Difference Makers understand, is that board of education meetings are when board members have governance and policy-making authority, occurring once a month, twice a month, or whenever they are scheduled officially in a local community. Thus, it is very important to ensure that board meetings allow for the best decisions to be made, utilizing sound, rational, and logical deliberation on items, with respectful discussion.

It is very important to ensure that board meetings allow for the best decisions to be made, utilizing sound, rational, and logical deliberation on items, with respectful discussion.

You might have guessed it. The superintendent's job is to ensure that each Difference Maker has what he or she needs to further those ends.

During board meetings, the environment must be inviting for all in attendance. The parking lots should be plowed and walks cleared. Does anyone greet people when they arrive? Someone probably should, and this could be a cheerful student or staff member. If the meeting is held in a school, we certainly hope that the public does not see the custodians still mopping the floors or emptying the garbage just prior to a board meeting.

We hope that, as board members, you have visibility with nameplates in front of where you sit, so that you can make a positive impression on the public. We also hope that you will encourage the superintendent to arrange your board table for optimal conversation. For example, the outside tables should angle inward just a bit, so that you all can talk with one another but also allow board members to face the public who are in the audience, without having to turn too much from one side to the other.

The board president should probably sit near enough to the superintendent that each can whisper to the other if needed. After all, these two are really the ones obligated to speak to members of the public at a meeting, more so than the entire group. They need space to compare notes and discreetly communicate.

Finally, it is entirely appropriate to expect that someone will be on hand to tend to any business needs the board might have, such as the need for copies made or for an extra writing utensil to be brought your way. This person could also help with technology or additional supplies as needed.

As Difference Makers, you will find that the best superintendents proactively tend to the monthly meeting setting in order to ensure that everything is available to make the best policy and governance decisions in a business setting.

Environment is key.

All About Relationships

While at board meetings, board members should be extra mindful of relationships and of offering unconditional positive regard for the members of the community who are visiting.

Hopefully, board members will come prepared, having their board packets read and their tasks done (paper shuffling), so that they can pay attention to people, not tasks, as things are getting started and while the evening is wrapping up.

As community members arrive, board members might wish to pay particular attention to who is paying attention to whom. The working-class dad should be provided the same level of respect and attention as the name-brand physician who chaired the last civic group fund-raiser. If board members do not treat people equitably, some members of the public *may* feel more valued than others.

The board must realize that, in the absence of mindfulness and intentionality, members may have a tendency to default to their favorites. Make sure you have a good plan for relationships with the public.

A good rule of thumb is to have board members divide up these tasks and ensure that each community member arriving (when practicable) is provided at least one positive affirmation by a board member. The superintendent and any others employed at the school can help with this as well. After all, those who feel good about themselves in visiting a place in which they may not be the most comfortable (i.e., community members visiting a school) may not find the need to take others down a peg or two in order to elevate their own status. It also gives people who *may have* been mistreated an opportunity to see that that was an exception and not the rule for our school system.

Basically, Difference Makers take every opportunity during those "down" moments in a public meeting to fill the space with an "all about relationships" goal, since it is only through the best of positive relationships that tasks get accomplished the most effectively.

It is only through the best of positive relationships that tasks get accomplished the most effectively.

Getting Down to Business

Board members don't want to waste one another's time or that of the superintendent or public. So it pays huge dividends to have someone running each board meeting in an efficient and effective manner. This is typically the responsibility of the board president.

Structures can be a board's best friend, such as that of the Consent Agenda, where more procedural items (and ones that can evoke a lot of meaningless rant) can be acted upon all at once. These could include approvals of minutes, acceptance of typical monthly reports, authorizing minor expenses, and the like. Think about how efficient things would be if you could lump ten, time-taking items at one fell swoop.

Bingo! It's done!

The beauty of a Consent Agenda is that, as board members, you can review these items ahead of time, and if you wish items to be moved to the Regular Agenda for further discussion, you can make that request as soon as the meeting starts. Difference Makers read thoroughly all of their documents in the board packet ahead of time so that they can be fully prepared and ready for input. Your superintendent should be providing this information in a clearly understandable, logically organized manner, with plenty of tabs and signposting.

And it is fair to request this information at least 48 hours in advance. Board members often have a "day job" and should not be expected to catch up with any new additions immediately before a board meeting. This sets up both boards and superintendents for potentially unwanted surprises. It is the superintendent's job to provide all of this information to the board with enough time for adequate review and consideration.

As a board, you'll want to get much business done in your board meeting before offering members of the community an opportunity for commentary. Community input can sometimes drag on, and it may even be uncomfortable. It also runs the risk of taking folks away from collaborative, productive conversation. So anything you can do to maximize the amount of healthy, amicable decision-making before contention enters the room is a good move. That said, don't hold off until midnight. That is probably a bit unfair and can bring out the

> As a board, you'll want to get much business done in your board meeting before offering members of the community an opportunity for commentary.

people who may have come with a particular issue to be in a worse mood than when they arrived. Additionally, it may seem like an intentional effort to avoid public input. Plus, most community members have to work in the morning.

One good strategy is to have two opportunities for public comment, one earlier in the meeting that allows for a specific number of minutes for each testimonial, and another later in the meeting. You want to provide a forum where the community feels "heard" but, again, one that is not a town hall meeting. Board meetings are meetings of a public governing body for getting done the business of a school district. They are not town halls.

From time to time, you'll need a closed-door, or "executive session," in which you might need to discuss sensitive items, such as employee performance evaluations, pending litigation, or even situations concerning the discipline of students. We recommend that you do this near the end of the meeting, so that people are not left stewing uncomfortably in the hallway outside. Some boards, however, find that holding a short executive session prior to each board meeting (such as the half hour before) allows for great efficiency, as board members can get some things discussed and have an established time frame for doing that.

It is important for board members to understand what an executive session is and what it isn't—what can be accomplished and what is, in fact, breaking sunshine laws. It is important that public bodies and officials deliberate in public. Board decisions (unless regarding school safety, HR issues, private student matters, to name a few) cannot happen in private.

The structure of board meetings and how you, as Difference Makers, conduct yourselves in public require good business practices and healthy discussions. The meetings are not town hall events or public bloodlettings where every adult with an opinion has the right to filibuster.

The structure of board meetings and how you, as Difference Makers, conduct yourselves in public requires good business practices and healthy discussions. The meetings are not town hall events or public bloodlettings where every adult with an opinion has the right to filibuster.

That said, keep in mind that typically the only one expected to respond to public concerns is the board president with help from the superintendent. You're not all on the line, unless you accept that or allow it. This is important for board presidents to communicate to other members in preparation. With only one or two voices (including the superintendent), the result is that the board sends no conflicting messages and is acting as one body, not as individuals reacting as they draw from the hip without full information.

Remember as well that, when faced with comments or criticism, you may simply wish only to thank folks for their comment and contribution as well. And then move on.

Good board presidents, as Chief Difference Makers, will offer members of the community assurances that they have been "heard" and that the leadership will do whatever it can to look into this or that and will bring the board an update on what they find, along with an amicable resolution when possible.

Our best board presidents realize that the *how* of public communication supersedes the *what*. They might even find that you can say just about anything to someone else when mindful of the delivery. During these exchanges, everyone must keep in mind that a board member's nonverbal communication will do more to elevate—or degenerate—a conversation than will anything else.

Board meetings are generally not the place for optimal discussion of problems, even though they naturally find their way there, especially if the problem involves contentiousness. These things should be resolved in private, and the board meeting should (most of the time) be a united and harmonious experience for attendees. Even the most dysfunctional families have an informal dynamic for behaving when there is company.

Hopefully, when your meetings close and you as a Difference Maker drive home, you consider the evening spent at school well worth your time, talent, and contribution. We hope you feel great about your leadership and are proud of what you said and did, while making a difference.

✅ Difference-Making Tips

◆ Difference Makers ensure that most items at a board meeting are organized efficiently by the superintendent and board president so that members of the public are best served and the business of the district is carried out. They strive to avoid bird walking and inefficiency.

◆ Difference Makers study their board packets carefully. If they have concerns they wish to express, they will inform the board president prior to the meeting, who can then reach out to the superintendent or encourage board members to do so directly. The key is that no "surprises" occur during the meeting, if possible.

◆ Difference Makers are effective at making good recommendations for board action and knowing which items need action and which need more investigation or study. They trust their board president and superintendent to be their barometers here, so that actionable items have been vetted through careful study and wise consideration.

10

Between Board Meetings

One board member's thoughts . . .

I realized early on in my board tenure that there's good reason for open meeting laws that restrict what can be said and done when you have more than a few board members in the same location outside of the regular meeting.

I'd bet the return on the investment of time is tenfold in a coffee shop sidebar.

Note to self: Spend more time in sidebars, legally.

There's a natural tendency to give a well-deserved *exhale* after any big evening or big event, taking a much deserved respite from all the ramp-up and excitement to pause and reach equilibrium once again.

This happens after our big board meetings as well.

After all, with all of the preparatory reading, late night studying, and the natural apprehension that goes with having to make the bigger and sometimes unpopular decisions in the business of school governance, who's going to blame you for wanting a brief reprieve from the activities before the exercise starts all over again.

We understand.

Yet true Difference Makers keep the exhale *right-sized* and short in duration, as there is a lot to expect from our boards of education between board meetings, as well as during them. And it is critical to note that you need to expect much from your superintendent between board meetings as well.

For it is between board meetings that our most powerful opportunities at local school district governance can take place, where the most "real" business oftentimes gets done (even though not publicly). And it is certainly where you can use both your influence within the community and your positive relationship with your superintendent to gain the most traction for your school district in a way that will advance the causes in which you believe.

It is between board meetings that our most powerful opportunity at local school district governance can take place, where the most "real" business oftentimes gets done.

We encourage a three-tiered strategy shared by board members and superintendents, so that difference making can be maximized between the official business sessions conducted with a gavel.

First, please be aware that your superintendent might and probably should reach out to you between meetings for some casual conversation and a request for your thoughts, feelings, or opinions on what is happening in the schools. This may or may not be something exactly aligned with the board committee upon which you sit or your role as secretary, treasurer, and so on but simply an opportunity to make contact with someone on the governance team, "just because."

Oftentimes, it's just because the superintendent wants to run something by someone who has a 10,000-foot perspective, and that is *you*. It might even be more personal in nature, and it could be that your superintendent simply wants to connect on a more informal basis, just to see how things are going. We hope you find that to be acceptable as well, and consider it a compliment to be called.

You should expect that your superintendent is intentional about getting to know you as a person as well as a governing board member and that this attempt to connect on a more personal basis is not an attempt to manipulate, as much as it is an opportunity to help better understand you in terms of how you wish to make a difference.

If you feel you are not consulted often enough, please let your superintendent know privately and confidentially what it is you need to feel that you are informed about and in the loop. There is nothing wrong with your sharing your wishes and expectations.

Second, we ask that you keep your ear to the wind about how the folks you know are perceiving your superintendent's job in the community, and, more so, we would hope that you would be so kind as to discreetly whisper in your superintendent's ear and let him or her know. What you'll want to see here is that those whom you respect and serve are feeling that their needs are being met and that their children and initiatives are in good care.

Think about it this way: Wouldn't you want your superintendent to be working hard for those whom you represent—actually, to be spending real hours each week being accessible and visible to those who go to you for support? Of course, you do. Your people deserve some of the superintendent's time and attention, so keep a watch to ensure that this is taking place and give leadership the heads-up when it isn't being perceived as such. The key is to have no surprises in the relationship.

And . . . When you catch your superintendent "being good" (visible and connected), don't be afraid to say so. Oftentimes the superintendency is a lonely job, and one in which there aren't too many confidants and trusted folks who let them know if they're spending time wisely on the things that matter. The interesting thing about serving as a positive confidant is that, when superintendents hear they are doing things right, they typically continue doing things similarly. It is simply a result of positive reinforcement. Think what a difference you could make for those you love and serve if all you had to do was pass along a friendly stroke to the superintendent when she or he does things as your constituency feels they should be done.

That's one of your *big* jobs between board meetings if you want to be getting more mileage out of your district leaders. It's when your superintendent can be seen authentically connecting and helpful to your constituencies that you know that your values align with your superintendent's and that opportunities are being created for those you care about.

Finally, we suggest to you as a Difference Maker that, given your busy schedule, when your superintendent does reach out to you once or twice each school year on a more formal basis—for a breakfast, luncheon, coffee, or the like—that you take time to meet and talk, especially in times when the both of you might not be on the same page. During these times, ensure that the superintendent is striving for professional/personal balance. Encourage personal wellness, and model it.

There is also real value in creating a few check-ins within your community to reflect with yourself as a board member once or twice a year. Here, you're not really spilling beans about board matters, governance, and other matters; rather, you are intentionally reaching out to a few people whom you already have a relationship with, whom you respect, and who have sound, clear judgment, to see how they are doing.

Check-ins will provide a good gauge to measure people's perceptions of how things are going within your community and school system. Of course, this needs to be done cautiously, as they don't know they are your sounding board or that you are auditing their perceptions.

These conversations can ground you, as it can be easy, as a member, to have the curse of knowledge regarding what is *really* going on. You can really use a few people who do not get caught up in the little stuff—or the big stuff—who can have balanced views, and who don't draw upon emotions.

The squeaky wheels often get the oil, but nonsqueakers can be just as important to hear from.

The squeaky wheels often get the oil, but nonsqueakers can be just as important to hear from.

These opportunities to connect are critical. They are great opportunities for you to get right to the business of governing effectively, as it is where the real business of school governance gets done, if we are to be honest. It's when local power brokers, such as yourselves, sit down one-on-one and "talk shop," *without* local reporters or the PC (politically correct) police within earshot. That said, just do a 360-degree turn to see who is within earshot before you let down your guard, as someone is often closer by than we would like.

And darn, that social media!

These meetings ideally last no more than an hour or so of your time—at are *your* convenience and in a location where you can share openly; they will very much allow you to get at the heart of whether or not you have someone to help *you* to make a difference. If you find that you are connecting better with your superintendent after your "real" conversations are held privately and semiannually, then we can assure you that your between-board-meeting time is being spent wisely.

The main point of this chapter is to remember that Difference Makers minimize the "exhale" after the *big meeting* and then consider each next day's best work between board meetings as helping considerably your next meeting's agenda. And the superintendent must minimize the exhale as well—as an opportunity for empathy on both sides, while the drum of governance and leadership keeps beating all the time!

And while visiting with others in one-on-ones and as we share with our school leaders, if your superintendent is doing a good job, please never miss the opportunity to make use of the power of a well-placed compliment. Every time we receive a compliment, we have a tendency deep down inside to think the person giving it is just a little smarter. It needs to be sincere, of course. Don't we want our superintendents to think that of us, as we make a difference?

Let's always look for the good things in our superintendents, even if sometimes we have to squint in the process. We might be pleasantly surprised in the good hiring decision we have made if we take the time to connect, caucus, and "be real."

✔ Difference-Making Tips

♦ Difference Makers know that what happens between board meetings is even more critical than what happens *at* each meeting of the board. This is partially because everyone seems to bring to each official gathering the cumulative emotions that have built up since the last meeting, positive or negative. Difference Makers help superintendents and superintendents help Difference Makers with emotions management.

◆ Difference Makers know that between-meeting activity is critical to having a functional board and administration, to keeping all focused on the 10,000-foot view, and to trusting the motives of one another. We would also encourage board members to do the same with one another—of course, being careful not to create a quorum. This is sometimes done easily after a previous scheduled administrative committee meeting. A deliberate check-in at least once a year with all board members (especially if you are board president!) is a good way to connect with and to keep up relationships and respect for one another.

◆ Difference Makers embrace opportunities to chat with superintendents between monthly meetings so that their superintendents can show them what their leadership is really all about and whether or not their vision is aligned in a way that connected and respected constituencies would support.

◆ Difference Makers will sit down individually with superintendents and try to work out differences, making the subject of the conversation what the conversation should *really* be all about. They are transparent with what they want and do not hide agendas while professing otherwise. They are not wolves in sheep's clothing.

◆ Difference Makers are very careful with social media between board meetings. They respect the online community but gauge it with caution. What seems like a political online storm might have no real movement behind it. Or it could.

11

Community Caricatures

One board member's thoughts . . .

I wonder who I would be if I were depicted as a caricature.

After all, we are caricaturized by others, oftentimes in a less flattering way than we would illustrate for ourselves.

I'd prefer something tactful, good-looking, levelheaded, and wise.

Note to self: We are oftentimes illustrated with the same pen as those we are seen commiserating.

In *The Secret Solution: How One Principal Discovered the Path to Success* (Whitaker, Miller, & Donlan, 2013, 2018), people employed in typical American schools were brought to life through parable. A parable is like a fable and can sometimes be a bit corny, but it does include some deep messaging and typically a big takeaway. In this case, it was a story of new Principal Roger Rookie of Anytown Middle School, who was quick to meet three distinctively different groups of teachers: the Superstars, the Fence-Sitters, and the Bullies.

Characters such as Lavon Babble, Edgar Sleeper, and Carl Chameleon were there, as were Sandy Starr and Nellie Newcomer. What these characters depicted were archetypes—those who behave in predictable ways across and among various contexts of life. We see typical archetypes every time we go to buy a car, renew a driver's license, or shop at the grocery store.

As board members serving in school governance roles, we see these archetypes in our school districts as well.

Think of Gabby Gossip and Socia Media and their influence on board policy and those monthly open community sessions. What about Axel Athletic when the fieldhouse is being discussed and Halie Helicopter when the assistant principal has disciplined students from a certain zip code? Marge Micro is elevated to board president after a superintendent squanders public money, and Yogi Union wins in a landslide when teachers are upset.

What Difference Makers such as yourself know about these roles is that, while appearing rather omnidirectional on the surface (one-plank wonders), something actually exists more deeply within their personalities. We can find what that is if we actually spend time to understand that the issue they are bringing to the board isn't really *what* they are bringing to the board.

There's typically another story. And, to be quite frank, as a Difference Maker, your role is to use the *how* of the moment to let your board president and superintendent figure out what is really going on and what to do about it.

Here's why.

Do you ever wonder why some open sessions at board meetings are relatively easy to hold, and others feel like root canals? Similarly, isn't it the case that with some community members, you find that conversations go where you thought they might, and others take wrong turns, some over very deep precipices.

This doesn't make for good community relations, especially if these are your neighbors who might be the best folks in the world when you're not talking school business. But imagine how awful it would be if your present, elected (and unpaid) position as a school board member forever alienated you from those whom you have to see each weeknight and weekend and from those who might even watch your house when you are away on vacation—or *have* for the last ten years?

Again, what we are sharing here is that, as a board member, you'll want to understand what is important when dealing with community caricatures. Whether at a board meeting, when seeing people at the grocery store, or when dealing with them over the neighborhood fence, you should keep in mind the following:

1. *How* you say something to them is much more important than *what* you say;
2. That said, never promise them that you will "handle it" in terms of the *what* they are asking;
3. And finally, take advantage of your superintendent's role as the *shield* and ask for some cover to help with them.

And while superintendents are valuable resources, so are other board members. We believe that it is okay to call and check a perception or comment with another board member. It would also be wise to buddy up with board members who have opposing views. They often can see issues from different perspectives and help consider angles and approaches; they can give you angles and talking points—not to fix things but to help message. And they can help remind you that the board already discussed something, what the board has decided, or the process for any action or reaction.

Regarding 1: *How* You Say Something to Them Is Much More Important Than *What* You Say

We all have a doorway to communication that is our favorite door. It has to do with *how* people communicate with us. Every time people knock on our favorite doorway, we can hear them and are willing to open up to what they are saying (Kahler, 1996, 2008, crediting Dr. Paul Ware's work additionally, 2015). We also have another doorway to communication that seems as if it is nailed shut. When people knock, we don't really even hear them, as they are not communicating to us in a way that resonates. Communication occurs mostly and ideally through open doors (Kahler, 1996, 2008, 2015).

We have these communication doorways; our community members do as well. In actuality, our communication doorways are constructed in our personalities, and they are very much hardwired but can change over time.

Our community members provide us hints about the nature of their open doorways to communication by what they say to us and how they respond to us. Even more fascinating is that, when we use open communication doorways through the *how* of communication, we will oftentimes get a positive response, even if we're doing not much of anything to solve the *what* of their concern.

We encourage you to focus on the *how* of communicating with members of the public and redirect the *what* of community concerns to other persons, such as your board president and/or superintendent.

An example might be:

Community Member:	Do you mean to tell me, given the fact that I have spent three personal days from work over the past two weeks dealing with a 9th-grader who simply refuses to go to school because his teachers are out to get him, that you cannot address this as a board?!
Board President:	Ms. Hardlee, thank you for taking your time in support of your son and for having the commitment to him in being here this evening. Do I understand it correctly that something is happening in school that is of much frustration to your son and that it is taking a toll on both him and your work schedule?
Community Member:	Absolutely. This didn't happen last year in middle school, and I am at the point where the constant struggle is affecting my job and our entire household. What can you do to address this? His teachers are out to get him! And I can prove it, if you would take a look at these remarks on his paper.
Board President:	Please know, Ms. Hardlee, that, as board president, I take your concerns seriously, as does the board. And your son's success in school and that of all students are foremost in our minds. May I ask at this time that you contact

the high school office tomorrow morning and share your work schedule with them. This will allow them to schedule a meeting for you and your son's teachers that will not require you to miss any more work. If you find that it is difficult coordinating schedules with the teachers, then I would suggest you connect with someone at the school who can help, such as our high school counselor. Would you be willing to place that call and, as well, to mention that you had taken your personal time this evening to make this presentation at our board meeting?

Community Member: Oh, I'll call tomorrow morning, but I'm doubtful that anything will be done about it. Just like nothing is being done about it this evening. What is the purpose of this board if it is not advocating for the children it serves?

Board President: Please know that what we are hoping to accomplish for you and your son, Ms. Hardlee, is really the best advocacy we can provide as a board. We want to advocate for you and the school to work together on the problem that is occurring. We don't see it as a situation that is too big for us to overcome together. Will you at least give our recommended path a chance? If it does not work, then you can always move to the level of a conversation with the principal, or even that of the superintendent if it cannot be solved at the building level?

Community Member: Oh, I'll be calling tomorrow morning, but I think I'll probably be back here next month. So, with that, have a good evening.

Board President: Thank you, Ms. Hardlee, and please know we hope all goes well when you, your son, and teachers sit down together. Have a good evening.

What this community member needed, in terms of communication, was recognition for her work and convictions (Kahler, 2008). This is demonstrated in Kahler's Process Communication Model® (PCM), which we recommend for those interested in a deeper dive on these subjects; however, what we can say here is that if board members are not focusing intently on the *how* of communication, you'll quite possibly end up using a closed doorway with one of these community members. This could run the risk of your losing friends, alienating your customers, or raising the ire of your neighbors when your children play together. It's just not worth it. Nothing productive is likely to come as a result.

So the best way to handle community caricatures is, again, by focusing on *how* you're going to hand off this conversation to someone else—like your *shield*—and work on a few specific deliveries that will work to do "just that." A few specific ways to do that would be to say:

> Might I now ask our superintendent if he/she would be able to suggest next steps or appropriate school-level contacts for a conversation in the next few days? [Sup's name], what would be a good next step for [community member's name] to take?
>
> You know, our conversation regarding this topic has reminded me that our superintendent has worked through similar circumstances prior. May I ask, [Sup's name], if you would share the best way to contact your office, for some additional follow-up after this evening's meeting? These issues are important to us.

Regarding 2: Never Promise Them That You Will "Handle It" in Terms of the *What* They Are Asking

Remember that sometimes the issue may be something you will want to be involved in and that there is a chance that next time you will not. You might want to be a part of the discussion involving the football coach and the team's stagnant passing game, but you could just as well pass on the controversy regarding band uniforms.

Professional board members keep in mind how they should interact every day. Your official power occurs only during meetings, but your unofficial duties are 24/7.

Additionally, never, ever become a part of the rumor mill. Just listening to some people gives the impression that you agree.

Watch what you text to others!

Don't leave a "paper" (i.e., electronic) trail.

It is a fine line that every board member must be aware of. At times, you may have to step away from the conversation. That can be difficult if it is family member or friend, but it may even be more critical then. We have all played the game of telephone where one person shares a story with the next, and by the time the story gets around the circle, it is vastly different. Rumors operate just like this, and you do not want to be a part of that mill.

Regarding 3: Take Advantage of Your Superintendent's Role as the *Shield* and Ask for Some Cover to Help with Them

By professionally referring things to the proper administrator in the chain of command, it does allow the superintendent to act as a *shield* to protect your credibility. In this role, when we handle things appropriately, this shielding naturally occurs.

We discussed a handful of caricatures at the beginning of this chapter, and we are confident that we can see parts of them in people in our communities. Some may draw a chuckle, and others bring out some ire. That is natural. Hopefully, it can also serve as a reminder that it is important that we, as board members, work diligently to handle situations in an appropriate fashion, so that people do not see these caricatures in us.

The superintendent needs, at times, to provide a *shield* for the board members. But please keep in mind that this is not a one-way relationship. By behaving in an appropriate manner, we can and must at times act as a *shield* for the superintendent.

A weakness in one can lead to a weakness in all.

And it bears keeping in mind that a superintendent will have a hard time pleasing every member on every issue that the

We cannot really change the hardwiring inside other people, so we might as well learn to make good connections with it.

community brings before the board. So board members can go a long way by cutting the superintendent some slack.

One takeaway regarding our community caricatures is that we cannot really change the hardwiring inside other people, so we might as well learn to make good connections with it. Doing so will bring out the best selves in everyone so as to provide connections and open doors of communication through which to listen to one another.

✔️ Difference-Making Tips

♦ Difference Makers see the positive things in community members' personalities and recognize that the *how* of conversation must be prioritized over the *what* of the conversation's content. The *what* is oftentimes better solved by school leadership, and the *how* allows for patience during this tactful redirection. A good strategy is to practice saying empathetically to a complainant, "How did the [school official] respond when you shared that [aggrieved person] was upset about [the situation]?" And, "Is there anything I can do to put you in touch with [school official]?"

♦ Difference Makers first strive to understand how they are being perceived while under pressure and to avoid misfiring themselves when uncomfortable topics are broached. They rehearse appropriate responses that they can use when surprised, offended, or uncomfortable. They do this to the point of muscle memory—cerebral muscle, that is.

♦ Difference Makers understand that if they are quick to react or grandstand at board meetings, then they will rapidly be seen as caricatures themselves, oftentimes unflattering ones. These depictions will last long after their tenure on the board ends and will follow them into other areas of service or community contribution. Given this, they are mindful of the images they project as they govern.

References

Kahler, T. (2008). *The Process Therapy Model: The Six Personality Types with Adaptations*. Little Rock, AR: Taibi Kahler Associates.

Kahler, T. (1996, 2015). *The Process Communication Model® Seminar: Seminar One/Core Topics*. Hot Springs, AR: Kahler Communications.

Whitaker, T., Miller, S., & Donlan, R. (2013). *The Secret Solution: How One Principal Discovered the Path to Success*. Lanham, MD: Rowman & Littlefield Education.

Whitaker, T., Miller, S., & Donlan, R. (2018). *The Secret Solution: How One Principal Discovered the Path to Success*. San Diego, CA: Dave Burgess Consulting.

12

Governing *Best*: Advancing by Retreating

One board member's thoughts . . .

I read once that, as much as we ask people to improve their shortcomings, they really can't do it all that well.

As a board member, I wonder what I'm perceived to have in terms of weaknesses.

Might some training this year help me to figure this out?

And if I get some training . . .

Am I willing to accept the answer and to do something to compensate for it?

Note to self: Take a step backward to move forward.

We have found that school boards across the country have members with the best intentions and great talent and yet that, at times, tend to the "normal curve" of average group performance in terms of how their talents combine.

We might ask ourselves, "How can an entire group function less well than the sum total of the talents of its individual members?"

On the flip side, "How can we move beyond average team performance to make the sum of the parts greater than the whole?"

First of all, we need to become students of performance enhancement.

We would note that performance enhancement involves a deep understanding of communication, leadership, motivation, talent management, psychology, and one's own work/life balance.

> **Governing at its best demands we recognize when one's contributions are serving as assets to the group and when they are serving as liabilities.**

Governing at its best demands we recognize when one's contributions are serving as assets to the group and when they are serving as liabilities. And this doesn't happen without a brief respite for "learning."

It demands *retreating* to student status every once in a while.

Yes, retreating before advancing.

Advancing by retreating.

Advancing by retreating, through quality school board professional development, allows board members to understand better not only the information presented to them to govern but, even more so, the dynamic through which they make decisions given that information.

Let's focus first on the latter.

While board members can have good individual intentions, the group can at times lack an understanding of how it can benefit from making decisions with input from those contributions collectively. For example, let's say that curricular changes are being considered with limited dollars to invest in materials. One member might understand gifted and talented programming; another knows intimately the value of athletics beyond the classroom. Another is an arts-infusion expert, while another sees clearly the need for numerical thinking taught across the curriculum. Yet does the group know how to put this all together without individual perspectives bumping into one another?

And, further, when is one's perspective really the best answer on how to move forward?

We often say that a healthy marriage should tend toward a 50/50 give-and-take. But that's not completely true, as sometimes one spouse must give 70% or even more to make things work . . . at least for a time or in one or two circumstances.

The same is true on a board of education of, let's say five members. Simple math would mean that each person could contribute a 20% perspective to yield optimal decision making that would be a result of the blended perspective. But, in actuality, an individual weight of 20% from each on that board would rarely yield a good decision. Sometimes a 20% outlier, even outnumbered, is really the one with the best answer. Not everyone's perspective is equally correct in board decision making; rather, almost everything is determined by context and resources.

So how can boards of education learn to make the best decisions, given a very dynamic theater of operation? How can the more introverted members step up and out of their comfort zones, away from conceding to the group's vote, to vocalizing their unique perspective? And, conversely, when is too much, too much, when those with stronger personalities are blind to their biases?

If we want boards of education to understand what to do with the information they receive and *how* to govern effectively, we suggest annual retreats and, from time to time, professional development (with state associations if they are available) to bring us back to School Board Governance 101. Life often gets so busy that we forget that boards of education must become the community's best students on what it means to serve on a board in the first place.

> **Life often gets so busy that we forget that boards of education must become the community's best students on what it means to serve on a board in the first place.**

We offer the following topics and potential discussion points for you all, as you advance while retreating:

Prompt One: Our Existence and Job Description as a School Board

We would suggest that school boards exist to represent the public who funds the schools. Boards represent the public taxpayer, not necessarily the parents. Said differently, public taxpayers might include business owners, parents, even school employees, and others, but boards are responsible to whoever foots the bill. And those folks are those who pay the money to keep the lights on, the buses running, the staff employed, and the curriculum delivered to students. Wouldn't it be interesting to have this conversation at your next board retreat? How would being responsible to taxpayers look differently than being responsible to students?

Prompt Two: Questions for Ourselves and Our Superintendent

We would suggest that school boards that ask how things are being done operationally are asking the wrong questions. Those that ask how things are being taught are probably asking the wrong questions also. You see, those questions are best left to the superintendent and leadership/management team of principals, instructional coaches, and others. What the school board should instead be asking is, "How effectively are we doing what we are doing?" After all, the school board is the public steward of quality educational programming and services. It determines the *what*, not the *how* things are going to happen. Wouldn't it be interesting for the board to have a conversation on how its deliberations can be more about the assurances made in terms of customer service, client satisfaction, and product quality than in terms of the number of widgets and sprockets being used on the assembly line or the tools used to rivet things together?

Prompt Three: Changing Circumstances as a Governing Board

It used to be for many of us that we had a steady stream of clients by virtue of their zip code and street address. We had a monopoly on the students who attended, as well as the funding that came with them. Across the country, things are changing. Yet have we changed the way we have done business in order to change with the times? Might we be interested in talking about shifts in market share and the use of budgetary resources in terms of influencing supply and demand? Just what are we doing with the changing circumstances we now enjoy—or not?

Prompt Four: Exercising Governance Monthly and Publicly

What strategies can we use at each board meeting to accomplish the following: (1) focusing quality time on the true issues of board governance items to leverage student learning to the satisfaction of the public taxpayers, (2) ensuring adequate input from introverts on the board during these discussions, and (3) avoiding the tendency for board meetings from becoming administrative Question and Answer (Q&A) drivel, program fashion shows, or administrative report-outs better put in a memo. Related to the last point, it is good to have some points of pride in board meetings, along with reports, but where and when are boards actually engaging the experts in the room—among the administrator and among the board members? The sanctity of these conversations needs to be protected.

Prompt Five: Sharpening the Saw on Finance

A board's fiduciary responsibility is a foundational part of its community compact in school governance. Unfortunately, because of a lack of budgetary sophistication, conversations during monthly board meetings can more often revolve around the purchase of specific materials (who, what, and what for) than really anything important. Imagine if the board would see those questions as left for others to ponder? Consider the power of board governance if all board members would focus instead on the overall financial standing of the school district, annual revenue and expenditures, monetary projections based on changing revenue streams and growth projections, and leading the "business" of schools. Oh, and wouldn't it be optimal if a board finance committee would know which accounts were most vulnerable to misspending or misappropriation (this varies per state), so that these could be spot-checked from time to time rather than micromanaging all the accounts?

Prompt Six: The Organizational Chart

Board members are supposed to be the Federal Aviation Administration of quality school governance, so wouldn't it make sense for them to know what is showing up when superintendents look at the radar scanning the landscape of school operations. We would bet that board members would find interesting a quick primer on the district and building organizational charts, in terms of who reports to whom, as well as their areas of responsibility in terms of operations and outcomes. Now this can be shared as written information, of course, but it is *best* explained with context and story, so that board members can connect what they are responsible for governing with real stories about the importance of these positions and the relationships to one another, all in terms of community outcomes for schools. This is really helpful for board members when they get calls and/or complaints from parents and community members in evenings, so that they can speak knowledgeably when they redirect callers to those who can help them in the quickest and best way.

Retreats as Key Professional Development Opportunities

Advancing by retreating is our way of making a plea for quality professional development for our nation's board members. Not only is this modeling critical for administration and leadership at all levels, including teachers and support staff, regarding the importance of continual training and self-improvement, but it can serve to enhance board member self-efficacy in their roles and will allow for more enjoyment given the vast responsibilities that they have.

We might say our best trained boards of education serve as a well-trained SWOT team in two senses of the word. First of all, in terms of how they envision strategic planning, board members are better able to perform a SWOT analysis—in terms of the strengths, weaknesses, opportunities, and threats—of what the district has, is, and will encounter in the retreat setting. That's SWOT in one sense of the word. Yet, metaphorically, boards of education retreat to advance, as well. Like a SWAT team in the world of tactics, they are asked to:

◆ Understand and respect the mission;
◆ Capitalize upon individual talents and strengths;
◆ Share a common focus;
◆ Establish clear lines of involvement;
◆ Execute with tight choreography;
◆ Refrain from operating where other units are assigned.

✔ Difference-Making Tips

◆ Difference Makers understand that their governance effectiveness is amplified by shared experiences of professional development. They carve out time from busy schedules to become "students" of board service, learning new things that may or may not have immediate practical significance.
◆ Difference Makers set goals for themselves while participating in training because, without goals (new and refined), there can be no advancement. These goals are not the annual goals that they have for their superintendents or school districts but rather goals that they have for their own professional and community performance.
◆ Difference Makers reflect on their professional learning at future meetings, so as to deepen the understanding they have of topics discussed and skills learned. They take the time to exercise these new ideas in monthly governance conversations that are at a board level, not to degenerate into administrative reports, program fashion shows, or the Q & A of leadership.

13

Starting Undefeated

One board member's thoughts . . .

Wow! A "re-DO"?!

I don't get that in my day job.

Note to self: Get some mileage out of it.

The profession of education and thus the opportunities for governance in education are special in that they provide do-overs. We have clear starting opportunities at the beginning of each academic year and well-defined ending points, such as when summer vacation (or any vacation, really) begins. These naturally occurring breaks allow for the revitalization of both energy and effort as we work to do better than we did the prior semester, to serve more effectively than we did the last time around.

We literally can reinvent ourselves.

Think about how the superintendents and principals in our schools use the new year as a way of establishing different expectations for students and teachers and even sometimes for parents and families as well. Teachers change the way they handle their lesson planning or provide for proactive classroom management, or at least we hope they do. Each new season is a prime time to influence the climate and even, little by little, to leverage a school or school district's organizational culture forward positively.

Are boards of education taking these prime opportunities to reinvent their governance each cycle or each year as well?

We certainly hope so.

You deserve it.

Reinvention is our chance to bring about true and lasting change to our school districts.

Reinvention is our chance to bring about true and lasting change to our school districts by planning for it first of all and also by modeling how the people in the highest levels of decision making take the opportunity to pause, reflect, hold up a mirror to what you do and how you're doing it . . . and then choose to make improvements.

And this is so important for boards of education to do, considering that the field of education itself is always reflecting, evaluating, considering best practice, new information, new data—the very system boards are elected to steer is foundationally set up to learn and then implement. Lifelong learning requires adding on to existing context and moving toward the next best direction. Boards would be liable for a type of malpractice, it would seem, if they were to intentionally *not* move forward or seek improvement.

In business and industry, leaders are not accorded these same opportunities, at least not so regularly. Many of you as business owners and employees know how difficult it is in those circumstances to breathe new life into what you are doing, as in any given August or September, the days can feel the same.

You may have brought on 25, or 50, or 500 new employees in the past 12 months, yet in just a short period of time, the workforce becomes indoctrinated into the way business is done. It's hard getting a do-over when the calendar doesn't have any natural restart points, along with permission to reinvent everyone and what we do.

Schools are different!

And by virtue of their roles, *so are* boards of education!

In a typical board cycle, there are new officer elections, new local campaigns, and a call from the public we know and love for changes in how we govern . . . in what we value and prioritize. Knowing all of this, the best chance we will have as Difference Makers is when we *first* begin our roles and when we begin them anew each and every school year.

Yes, board structure is ripe for do-overs and for complete change too! Every time the group changes, even if only by one person, the whole dynamic and focus of the group can change. It presents the opportunity for generating so much energy. This keeps groups and systems fresh, and it builds capacity and is necessary for a thriving system.

The First Days of School

We often hear that classroom teachers must earn the respect of students in order to be successful. You want to know a secret? It's really not true.

Students typically behave very well when school starts each year.

Teachers are given a gift of folks in their places with bright, shiny faces. It's what they do next—*or not*—that either makes or breaks the rest of the year with those who are there, ideally, to learn.

It's *all* on the teacher.

This same applies to our school principals and superintendents, really. You know this, as you keep a close eye on what your district and building leaders are doing. And you hear it from your constituents.

When leaders first take their jobs, they are on their best behavior. Teachers and staff dress better; they show up for meetings on time. What your district and building leaders do from that point forward will not only establish a "new normal," but it will also create norms of success or norms of failure.

Imagine the new principal who listens to those who criticize faculty and staff and then arrives at the first staff meeting talking about how both the climate and culture need to improve from this day hence!!

Well, this principal not only doesn't really understand school culture but doesn't really know how to lead too well either. A wide net of aspersion has been cast over everyone—even the good folks—because of rumors pertaining to the "bad" folks, and our best, who are truly making a difference, are alienated.

This principal had a slim window to reinvent, as brief as it might have been, to enact positive change.

And blew it.

Superintendents are given this slim window as well with their leadership teams. And you evaluate them on how well they use it, don't you?

You as a board member have the same opportunity.

Are you grading yourself?

Taking stock in how you leverage the gift?

The natural do-over?

Whether or not you voted *for* or *against* your new superintendent, or even if you have a superintendent with a tenure of 20 years, think about the choice you have to start undefeated, each time the clock gives you the do-over in the profession of education.

And think who's counting on you to leverage that.

Think of it as *your* first day on the job.

After all, those who are friends and colleagues on your board really want you to succeed, if they're decent people, and you want the same for them. A time in which you are all able to start undefeated, anew, is really a great opportunity to help provide new and enlightened guidance to one another in how you can elevate your game of governance.

The strong will embrace and learn from it.

The weak and insecure will continue to use the groove of least resistance—that which feels comfortable.

The one-trick pony groove.

Friends, our roles are so complex, in an educational system that is constantly changing and is undergoing increased scrutiny by both legislative bodies and the public, that we will never stay undefeated in the eyes of everyone for very long. But, regardless, when we're given the opportunity to serve, children are depending on us, so we must do what is right.

When we're given the opportunity to serve, children are depending on us, so we must do what is right.

We must "default" to trying, and that means reinventing.

That is the only thing that will work out well for us over time.

It would be nice if our communities agreed with every decision we made. It would be wonderful if fellow board members agreed with every course of action we proposed, but that's just not reality.

So, with this the case, let's start undefeated every time we have the chance.

Children and community depend upon it.

✔ Difference-Making Tips

◆ Difference Makers realize that their first at-bat is their *only* first at-bat. Thankfully, they still have the opportunity to make home runs the remainder of their years on the board. And although they will never again have an opportunity to swing at that first ever pitch thrown to them as rookies, they will have another swing at *a* first pitch each year.

◆ Difference Makers realize that their governance earns a grade point average, just like students earn grade point averages. They know that their earlier grades from board service will have much more impact on later board service because they weigh more significantly. Thus, they "measure twice" before each cast of their vote.

◆ Difference Makers realize that, at the end of each week, semester, and year, they will never be without some mistakes. It is thus very important to start undefeated while they can and be known for the honor in how they played the game and humbly to ask for a re-do when appropriate. After all, everyone inducted into any hall of fame has a win/loss record. Most can write better books on what the losses taught them.

Epilogue: What Next?

So you have probably found that service as a member or officer of a board of education has given you a powerful opportunity to be a Difference Maker.

We believe that, for some of you, board service has given you an opportunity to apply science to your art. In other words, you were always good at this, and the officially elected local position has provided you a platform of empowerment to ensure that your great ideas are materialized into action.

Good for you!

We hope, as you finish this book and consider reading another, that something special will happen to you. That you will see appearing in front of you a new window of opportunity.

You now have an opportunity to make differences not just *for* your superintendents, principals, teachers, students, families, and communities but *through* these same folks.

Difference making best happens *through* other people, not *to* other people, and here is why.

Beyond difference making in a community and with community members—

Building (and existing within) strong boards requires an ability to view when they are at their best, when they are working together. A high-achieving board owes its success to positive group dynamics, respect for one another, a common interest in doing the right and best thing, and not needing to control every single vote and every decision. Great board members yield to others' wisdom, have confidence that it is okay to not know all the answers, and regard themselves as professionals.

This is not done accidentally.

This is done through intentional conversations that may take added work but show dividends in the long run.

Group dynamics within boards can make or break a board.

And within these so very important groups, "Many hands make light work," as the Irish proverb goes.

Difference Making is like offering a community well in which everyone can drink a bit from the performance-enhancing supplement of positive relationship building with an unconditional regard for others.

As board members, you are Difference Makers in Chief, and please know others are watching you do "just that," more closely than before you wore your title.

The Difference Maker

Consider this: Your core incentive to engage in public service was to make a difference. Even if you have taken the same path as others on your local school board to get here, you have arrived at the same place.

Now on the board, why would you want simply to make time pass or merely attend monthly meetings? Conversely, why would you want to be *so* involved in everything that you are so incredibly busy and worried about minutiae that you never really get to advance your causes because you're too busy trying to make a difference in what others are employed to do?

The sweet spot of difference making is really an easy formula:

1. Embrace difference making.
2. Learn a board of education's true role.
3. Let your superintendent lead and manage.
4. Understand constituencies.
5. Use the *shield* you are provided.
6. Care for and feed your community.
7. Serve effectively *between* board meetings.
8. Embrace community caricatures, and focus on *how* you respond.
9. Enjoy your tour of duty.
10. Advance by retreating.
11. Start undefeated.
12. Focus on adults in schools *first* and on children *most*.
13. And be OK with all that.

We have chosen, as members of boards of education, to affect positively the generations who will live past us, who will raise children of their own. We want to leave legacies that last far beyond us. In order to do so, we must align making our difference with doing the right thing. By choosing wisely and once we internalize these connections, we will live our lives as Difference Makers.

Not for us, but for others.

For children and families.

That is why we selected service on a school board.

That is why we choose to govern.

That is why we hire superintendents, evaluate them rigorously, set budgets, listen to our community, and refrain from trying to run things.

Just as we expect others to do their jobs, we also have to provide paths for ourselves to do the same. At the end of the day, we know we are in the right place in local service when we look in the mirror and see that governance at 10,000 feet is a bit more tiring than many give it credit for.

Perhaps that is our greatest gift: staying at 10,000 feet but providing a close watch on the theater of operation, making opportunities, providing second chances to others and ourselves, reinventing education, and, of course, . . . making a difference.

Thanks for what you *do*.

Our children deserve it.